C000183852

Notes from a
SCEPTICAL
GARDENER

Notes from a
SCEPTICAL
GARDENER

MORE EXPERT ADVICE FROM
THE *TELEGRAPH* COLUMNIST

KEN THOMPSON

The Telegraph

ICON

Published in the UK in 2020
by Icon Books Ltd, Omnibus Business Centre,
39–41 North Road, London N7 9DP
email: info@iconbooks.com
www.iconbooks.com

Sold in the UK, Europe and Asia
by Faber & Faber Ltd, Bloomsbury House,
74–77 Great Russell Street,
London WC1B 3DA or their agents

Distributed in the UK, Europe and Asia
by Grantham Book Services, Trent Road,
Grantham NG31 7XQ

Distributed in the USA
by Publishers Group West,
1700 Fourth Street, Berkeley, CA 94710

Distributed in Canada by Publishers Group Canada,
76 Stafford Street, Unit 300
Toronto, Ontario M6J 2S1

Distributed in Australia and New Zealand
by Allen & Unwin Pty Ltd,
PO Box 8500, 83 Alexander Street,
Crows Nest, NSW 2065

Distributed in South Africa by
Jonathan Ball, Office B4, The District,
41 Sir Lowry Road, Woodstock 7925

Distributed in India by Penguin Books India,
7th Floor, Infinity Tower – C, DLF Cyber City,
Gurgaon 122002, Haryana

ISBN: 978-178578-637-2

Typeset in Adobe Caslon by Marie Doherty

Printed and bound in the UK by Clays Ltd, Elcograf S.p.A.

CONTENTS

Practical gardening

On being a gardener

ABOUT THE AUTHOR

Ken Thompson was for 25 years a lecturer in the Department of Animal and Plant Sciences at the University of Sheffield. He recently retired and moved to Devon, and writes regularly on gardening for the *Daily Telegraph*. His book, *Where Do Camels Belong?* (Profile, 2014), was described as 'lively and punchy' by the *Sunday Times*, and the predecessor to this volume, *The Sceptical Gardener* (Icon, 2015), was hailed as 'a delight' by *The Spectator*. In 2016 he was awarded the Royal Horticultural Society's Veitch Memorial Medal for his contribution to the advancement and improvement of the science and practice of horticulture.

INTRODUCTION

Sport goes on and on, you see. You have to run on the spot to keep up. Events just keep on coming: moreover they keep coming in exactly the same order, year after year, which is sensible, but also a bit depressing if the sporting calendar's rigid cycle dictates your actual life.

Lynne Truss in *Get Her Off The Pitch!*
How Sport Took Over My Life

In the above quote, Truss is explaining why, after four years, she had had enough of being a sports correspondent for *The Times*. I'm sure she's right about sport, but gardening, if anything, is even worse. At least when Spurs play Chelsea this year, the result may be different from last year; the exact score is almost certain to be. But it's hard to persuade yourself that planting your runner beans or pruning your wisteria this year will feel much different from the same job last year. And gardening journalism can feel the same; once you've written one column on 'what to do in June', do you ever need to write another one?

Thus it was, ten years ago, that I set out to write a different kind of gardening column. One that addressed questions with no obvious answer – or worse still, answers that are all too obvious, but still turn out to be wrong. One that asked questions that no one in their right mind had even bothered to ask before, such as whether birds understand speed limits, whether foxes really are getting bigger, what (if anything) the plants on the Duchess of Sussex's new coat of arms tell us, and just what are 'plants' anyway? Occasionally, I even write something useful, such as how to make your own slug gel, the best way to stop the needles falling off your Christmas tree, or the best plants to persuade someone to buy your house.

My indispensable partner in this enterprise was, and still is, Joanna Fortnam, gardening editor of *The Daily Telegraph*. Joanna and I, despite actually meeting only rarely, manage to see eye to eye on the need for a column like mine – grit in the gardening oyster. Remarkably, ten years on, there still seems to be an inexhaustible supply of fresh stuff to ramble on about, and even more remarkably, neither Joanna nor the readers of the *Telegraph* seem to have tired of those ramblings.

After about five years, the columns available at the time were collected in the book *The Sceptical Gardener*. And now, in what seems like no time at all, here we are again, with a completely fresh collection. As before, I have not attempted to update them. Most don't need it, and in any case the updating itself would soon be out of date. Here and there, I have added a brief footnote that explains where we are now (in late 2019). In even fewer cases, a footnote clarifies a topical reference that isn't obvious from the context. Otherwise, the columns are reproduced here in exactly the form in which they were originally written. A handful of columns failed, for one reason or another, to appear in the *Telegraph* (Joanna and I don't agree about *everything*), but it seems a shame to waste them (especially as one or two are personal favourites), so they're here too.

A huge thank you to Joanna, of course, for putting up with me all this time. And also to Duncan Heath at Icon Books, who not only took a chance on publishing the first collection, but was happy to come back for more. To everyone else at Icon, including Ellen Conlon for her work on the text, Marie Doherty for her typesetting, Lisa Horton for her lovely cover design, and Ruth Killick for publicity, and to Michael Stenz at the *Telegraph*, for seeing the project through to fruition. Many thanks as always to my wife Pat for putting up with me while I write. Finally, thanks to you, the reader. If these columns are new to you, I hope you like them, and if you've read them before, I hope you enjoy them all over again. I certainly enjoyed writing them.

NAMES OF THINGS, MAINLY PLANTS

The fritillary's chequered past

Reading a magazine article recently, I was surprised to find 'marsh fritillary' included among a list of plants. I suppose if you were a plant person, familiar with the common snake's head and other fritillaries of the botanical sort, you might easily assume a marsh fritillary was a plant. In fact, of course, the marsh fritillary is a butterfly, and there are several other fritillary butterflies. Which set me wondering: why are the plants and the butterflies both called fritillaries?

The first thing to notice is that the butterflies and the snake's head fritillary (but not most other plant fritillaries) share a rather similar chequered pattern, black and orange in the butterflies and various shades of purple in the plant. There is a general consensus, shared by Wikipedia and my *Shorter Oxford Dictionary*, that the name refers to this pattern, and comes from the Latin *fritillus*, meaning dice-box. But what exactly is a *fritillus*, and what has it got to do with a chequered pattern?

Well, the Romans were great gamblers, and went to a lot of trouble to prevent players cheating when throwing dice. The simplest solution was the *fritillus*, which was more of a dice-cup than a dice-box – usually a fairly plain cylindrical container in which dice were shaken before being thrown. Often they had ridges or grooves on the inside to help to agitate the dice and further prevent any attempt to interfere with a fair throw.

2

But this is where things get complicated, because we have several *fritilli* recovered from Roman sites, and there's nothing remotely chequered about any of them. Maybe the answer is the *pyrgus*, or dice tower, the ultimate anti-cheating device. A *pyrgus*, which removed the human element entirely, was a square tower, open at the top. Dice are thrown into the top and descend past a series of baffles, eventually leaving the tower at the bottom, tumbling down a short staircase which mixes them up even more. As long as the dice are fair, the *pyrgus* completely prevents cheating.

OK, you're thinking, so what? Well, the dice tower had perforated lattice-work sides, probably to allow the players to see the dice inside, and make sure that the dice that left at the bottom were the same as the ones that went in the top. Overkill, you may think, but it looks like the Romans really did have a big problem with people cheating at dice. Crucially, this lattice pattern looks a bit like the chequered pattern of a fritillary, so maybe – just maybe – this is where the name comes from.

But then again, maybe not. In his book *Flora Britannica*, Richard Mabey prefers the account in John Gerard's famous *Herball, or Generall Historie of Plantes*, first published in 1597. According to Gerard, 'it hath beene called *Fritillaria*, of the table or boord upon which men play at Chesse, which square checkers the floure doth very much resemble'. Which certainly seems more straightforward than the tortuous dice-box story, although I should warn you that other theories are available; a variation on the *fritillus* story says that fritillary flowers resemble the *shape* of a *fritillus*.

We'll probably never know the truth for certain, although I like the Gerard story. Either way, the snake's head fritillary is both attractive and easy to grow, and will happily naturalise in a patch of damp grass. Beware the scarlet lily beetle, which likes to eat fritillaries, although the snake's head is usually just a bit too early to suffer any serious damage. But if you want to see a fritillary butterfly, you will have to make a special effort; the urban gardeners among you are unlikely to see any of our eight native species in your garden.

DNA opens a can of worms for gardeners

Whatever Marie Kondo* may have to say on the subject (and frankly, who cares?), the arrival of a new book in the Thompson household is always a cause for celebration.

---

* The author of the bestseller *The Life-Changing Magic of Tidying*, who famously asserted that no one needs more than 30 books.

Especially when it's the fourth edition of Clive Stace's *New Flora of the British Isles*.

Let me explain. For every generation, there's a standard British Flora; the book whose mission, in the words of the first edition, is simply to enable botanists to identify the plants found growing in the wild in the British Isles. Since 1991, that book has been what is universally referred to as 'Stace'. Pre-Stace, British Floras tended to be a bit sniffy about introduced plants, but Stace changed all that. Recognising that you often couldn't know whether an unknown plant was native or alien, or whether someone had planted it or not, the pragmatic approach was to include everything you might expect to find in the wild. And since *the* source of new wild plants in Britain, more important than all the others combined, is horticulture, Stace is a useful guide to garden plants too.

For Flora writers, and for botany in general, the seismic shift came between editions two and three. Previously, our ideas about how plants are related to each other had been based mostly on morphology, but plant classification has been revolutionised by molecular data, especially DNA. The third edition of Stace was the first to reflect that revolution. But the changes were far from complete, and in fact they still aren't, so although Stace's approach is essentially a conservative one, the new edition includes many new changes that are now clearly here to stay.

For gardeners, some of these changes are uncomfortable, to say the least. We already knew that *Hebe* had vanished into *Veronica*, and that most asters now belong in *Symphyotrichum*, but some changes go further than that. Sometimes, the genera created or altered by DNA information *are morphologically indistinguishable*.

To appreciate the true horror of that, you need to know that at the core of any Flora is a huge number of dichotomous keys, which lead you (with luck) via pairs of choices to the right name for the plant in front of you. Right at the start, a whopping great key takes you to a family. Once you're in the right family, another key takes you to a genus, and then a final one takes you to a species.

When the whole system was based on morphology, that worked a treat, and mostly it still does. But consider the fate of *Sedum*. Ever since Linnaeus, *Sedum* has always looked like a large group of species that are obviously closely related to each other. But, says the DNA, they're not. Old favourite *Sedum spectabile* is now *Hylotelephium spectabile*, and even two plants as similar as *S. spurium* and *S. rupestre* are now in different genera: *Phedimus spurius* and *Petrosedum rupestre*. As a result, Stace has abandoned a key to *Sedum*, and instead has a combined key to *Sedum* and the other three genera. Taxonomists don't like having to do this, but there really is no other option.

Sometimes, the problem arises in reverse: plants that

surely *must* be different but aren't. The DNA says that *Mahonia* and *Berberis* belong together, but don't panic; fearing a riot down at the garden centre, the taxonomists are doing everything they can to keep them apart.

Will the real laurel please stand up?

A while ago I came across a short article in a gardening magazine about laurels. It talked about Portuguese laurel (*Prunus lusitanica*) and spotted laurel (*Aucuba japonica*), but had most to say about cherry laurel (*Prunus laurocerasus*), which it described as 'the true laurel'.

My *Shorter Oxford Dictionary* defines a laurel as (among other things) both 'a tree or shrub of the genus *Laurus* (family Lauraceae), especially the bay tree, *Laurus nobilis*' (and, separately, as any member of the Lauraceae) and 'any of various trees and shrubs having leaves resembling those of the bay tree'. Which illustrates the problem; the word 'laurel' is being asked to do too much. On the one hand, it's shorthand for the bay tree, or any member of the genus *Laurus*, or indeed of the family Lauraceae. On the other hand, it's a useful name for any laurel-like tree or shrub, which essentially means anything with leathery, entire, evergreen leaves.

That second definition is very broad indeed, and can include several evergreen cherries and the spotted laurel (as above), plus spurge laurel (*Daphne laureola*), Alexandrian laurel (*Danae racemosa*), Chilean laurel (*Laurelia sempervirens*), two American oaks (*Quercus hemisphaerica*, *Q. laurifolia*), and no doubt others. Naturally the cherries are related to each other, but all the other laurels are completely unrelated, to each other or to *Laurus*. On top of that, there's the rest of the Lauraceae, including sassafras, cinnamon, avocado and *Lindera* which, unusually for a laurel, is deciduous and is grown mostly for its excellent autumn colour. The wonderful Californian laurel or headache tree (*Umbellularia californica*) has aromatic leaves, a bit like bay but even stronger – I never was quite sure whether the smell was supposed to *give* you a headache, or cure it. A very fine specimen in Sheffield Botanical Gardens blew down in a storm a few years ago, and is sadly missed.

In Ancient Greece, wreaths of bay laurel leaves were used to crown the victors of athletic competitions in the ancient Olympic games. Julius Caesar and Napoleon Bonaparte both understood the symbolism of the laurel wreath and liked to be pictured wearing one. And in modern times the laurel wreath lives on, even if only symbolically, in words like 'Baccalaureate' and 'Laureate'.

So where does that leave the 'true laurel'? On both botanical and historical grounds, I'd say that accolade belongs to the bay laurel. And I know I'm just prejudiced, but I would also say that the bay laurel is a better plant from a purely gardening perspective, as long as you can put up with its suckering habit. Cherry laurel is a thug, and spotted laurel is just plug ugly, although Portuguese laurel is a more refined shrub that deserves to be more widely grown. And spurge laurel is a lovely native plant for a shady spot, producing its inconspicuous and pleasantly (if faintly) scented flowers at a time of year when there's not much else to look at in the garden.

On the other hand, it's not my job (or anyone else's) to police the use of the word laurel, so if you agree with the author of my original article that cherry laurel is the 'true laurel', no one is going to stop you. But the next time anyone tells you they've planted a laurel (or even a true laurel), you're entitled to raise a questioning eyebrow.

Time's up for rosemary

As we learn more about the family relationships of plants, chiefly these days by looking directly at their DNA, we often find that our earlier ideas weren't quite right. One outcome is that plants' names need to change.

Mostly this means one of two things. One possibility is that we need new names. For example, the sprawling empire that was once *Aster* has nearly all vanished into new genera, and most of our garden Michaelmas daisies are now in *Symphyotrichum*. That had to happen, and my only complaint is that they could have chosen something easier to both say and spell. Something very similar has also happened to *Sedum*. This process is far from complete, so for example *Sorbus* (whitebeams and rowans) is currently on death row, and survives in its present form only because no one can decide what to do with it.

The second common outcome is the loss of familiar names, usually because one genus is found to be embedded within another, for example *Hebe* turns out to be entirely surrounded by *Veronica*. Leaving things like that would mean there were speedwells that were more closely related to hebes than they were to other speedwells, which is not allowed, so *Hebe* had to go. *Lavatera*, *Nectaroscordum*, *Saintpaulia*, *Chionodoxa* and many others have gone the same way.

The latest high-profile casualty is rosemary, which nicely illustrates the difficult decisions thrown up by the DNA evidence. There was always a good argument, purely on morphological grounds, for including *Rosmarinus* in *Salvia*, and the latest DNA evidence confirms that that's where it belongs. So far so good, but what to actually *do* about that isn't necessarily obvious. It may sometimes look like the botanists are out to confuse gardeners, but in reality they strive to make as few changes as possible, consistent with the scientific evidence.

In the present case, rosemary is in a branch of the *Salvia* family tree along with several other familiar salvias, including *Salvia officinalis* and *S. sclarea*. If you really wanted to, you could keep *Rosmarinus*, and those salvias, exactly as they are, but only at the cost of a version of the hebe/veronica problem: salvias more closely related to rosemary than they are to each other (definitely not allowed). And the only way out of *that* problem would be to invent a whole load of new genera for all the other salvias, such as the lovely *S. patens* and hundreds of others. Faced with the inevitability of upsetting an applecart, the botanists decided to upset a small one (*Rosmarinus*) rather than a large one (*Salvia*), a decision which I'm sure we can all applaud.

So rosemary is now *Salvia rosmarinus*, and we – and the manufacturers of plastic plant labels – are just going to have to get used to it. Of course, you can still call it rosemary, just as you can still grow hebes and asters, even if the plants are no longer in those genera.

Oh, I nearly forgot, exactly the same fate has befallen *Perovskia*, so *P. atriplicifolia* is now *Salvia yangii*. Why not *Salvia atriplicifolia*? Don't ask – that would be a whole other column, and a very dull one.

11

Better than wrong

Some time ago, I read some sensible advice on managing self-seeding garden plants, warning that although allowing self-seeders to grow is a great source of free plants, it can be problematic if you have weedy soil. Specifically: 'You can't take this laissez-faire attitude in a new or neglected garden, as the self-sown weeds choke the rest. Annuals such as groundsel, bittercress, bird's-eye speedwell and sour thistle appear among the interesting, planted things, and the place becomes hard to keep on top of. But if your soil is relatively clean of weed seed after several years of regular tidy-ups, then what germinates in spring is usually desirable.'

Excellent advice, but what caught my eye was 'sour thistle'. There's no such plant, and it's clearly a mis-hearing of 'sow thistle' (*Sonchus oleraceus*). On the other hand, sour thistle captures something that sow thistle doesn't, and you almost wish *Sonchus* really was called sour thistle. Is there, I wondered, a name for such things, i.e. mis-hearings that are at least as good as the original, and maybe even better? Before the internet, I might have gone on wondering, but Google answered my question right away. There is such a word, and it's far from new, with an interesting history.

In an essay in *Harper's Magazine* in 1954, American writer Sylvia Wright recalled how, as a young girl, she misheard a line from the 17th-century ballad 'The Bonnie Earl o' Moray':

> Ye Highlands and ye Lowlands,
> Oh, where hae ye been?
> They hae slain the Earl o' Moray,
> And laid him on the green.

She heard the last line as 'And *Lady Mondegreen*', liking the romantic image of the stricken Earl and the beautiful Lady Mondegreen dying in each other's arms. Thus was the word 'mondegreen' coined by Wright for a mistake that's better than the original.

A fertile source of mondegreens is song lyrics, which are often indistinct, and sometimes apparently meaningless even if you can hear them. I've spent my entire adult life believing that in 'Purple Haze', Jimi Hendrix sang "Scuse me while I kiss this guy', while all printed versions of the lyrics plainly say "Scuse me while I kiss the sky'. In my defence, I was far from alone in the mistake, and Hendrix acknowledged the frequent mis-hearing by often deliberately singing the 'mondegreen' version in concert.

Sometimes, the mondegreen eventually becomes the correct version. The original version of 'Twelve Days of

Christmas' has 'four colly birds', from the Old English *col*, meaning an ember or charred remnant, and thus meaning black, and eventually giving us the word coal. So the four colly birds are blackbirds. But sometime around the turn of the 20th century, colly fell out of use and they became calling birds, which is now the lyric of the official version.

But one of my favourite mondegreens is another plant. In his wonderful book *Flora Britannica*, Richard Mabey reports that the daughter of one contributor grew up believing that ivy-leaved toadflax (*Cymbalaria muralis*) was really called 'I believe in toadflax'.

GARDEN
WILDLIFE

Darwin meets the bird feeder

As I think I've mentioned before, bird feeding in British gardens takes place on a massive scale; the UK spends twice as much on bird seed as the rest of Europe put together. It would be surprising if this weren't having some large effects, not least on the birds themselves. A recent study by a consortium of British and Dutch researchers, and published in the journal *Science*, sheds some interesting light on the subject.

One of the commonest species at bird feeders is the great tit, and measurements of hundreds of specimens from museums in Britain and mainland Europe show that British great tits have longer beaks. The difference isn't enormous, but then neither are the beaks.

Of course, that in itself doesn't tell us very much. There are no known differences in ecology and behaviour between British and European great tits, but maybe our tits have always had longer beaks for some unknown reason, or just by chance. So the authors looked at data from one of the best-studied bird populations in the world – the great tits of Wytham Wood near Oxford. Twenty-three years of data from Wytham's birds show a steady increase in beak length. Again the change isn't large, only about 0.1mm, but that's a lot over such a short time, in an organ that only measured 13.5mm to start with.

But why are beaks getting longer in British great tits? The researchers found a gene, catchily named COL4A5, that was strongly linked to the change in beak length. They were then able to show that British birds with this gene successfully raised more fledglings, but that Dutch birds with the same gene did not. In fact, having the long-beak gene even seemed to be a slight disadvantage for Dutch birds. Notably, the greater success of the British birds wasn't because they laid more eggs, they were just more successful at turning eggs into fledgling birds. Which in turn suggests that longer-beaked birds may be managing to obtain more food.

Back to Wytham, where data from radio-tagged birds showed that the genetically-distinct, longer-beaked birds were more likely to use bird feeders. In other words, it looks like birds with the long-beak gene may somehow be able to get more out of bird feeders. But the researchers don't speculate about exactly how this might happen, so although the link between beak length and bird feeders looks plausible enough, more work is needed to figure out exactly what is going on. If our favourite theory turns out to be wrong, it wouldn't be the first time. Personally, given the recent news about admissions to Oxbridge, I wonder if having longer beaks doesn't just make it easier for Oxford's great tits to look down their noses at other birds.*

---

* A topical reference; former Labour education minister David Lammy had accused Oxford and Cambridge colleges of failing to offer places to black and ethnic minority candidates and those from less well-off backgrounds.

A footnote to this research is that the researchers identified a number of other genes connected to beak length, two of which are also linked to variation in beak shape in Darwin's finches, nicely connecting this example of natural selection right back to the origin of the concept. I also can't help noting that the *Science* paper reporting all this is entitled 'Recent natural selection causes adaptive evolution of an avian polygenic trait', a title that might have been designed to conceal this fascinating stuff from all but the most inquisitive reader.

Thumbs down for neonicotinoids

Neonicotinoids are systemic insecticides that inevitably find their way into pollen and nectar, and are thus consumed by bees, albeit in very low doses. You could be forgiven for thinking that the argument about whether this does the bees any harm would never end. Some experiments say it does, others say it doesn't, giving encouragement to both sides of the debate. But one thing is for sure: almost all previous studies have taken place under some kind of artificial conditions, rather than in the real agricultural world.

The manufacturers of neonicotinoids have always maintained that this lack of realism exaggerates the negative effects of neonicotinoids, and that in normal use they are safe. So, full marks to Syngenta Ltd and Bayer CropScience for putting their money where their mouth is and funding a massive new study, although by now they must be wishing they hadn't bothered.

The research, published in the journal *Science*, took place in the UK, Hungary and Germany, and was carried out here by the Centre for Ecology and Hydrology. Oilseed rape was grown under standard agricultural conditions, with all the usual pesticides and fertilisers. The only difference was that some of the rape was treated with the neonicotinoids clothianidin or thiamethoxam, and a control was not. The researchers measured the impact on honeybee hives and on colonies of a common bumblebee and a common solitary bee.

The effect on honeybees was inconsistent: negative here and in Hungary, but not in Germany. For the other two bees, there was no obvious effect of the experimental treatment. But fortunately, the researchers had taken the precaution of measuring the amount of neonicotinoids accumulated in the nests, which revealed a clear effect: nests with more neonicotinoids performed worse. Even more alarmingly, residues in nests didn't consist only of the clothianidin or thiamethoxam applied during the experiment; they also found a third neonicotinoid, imidacloprid. Since all three chemicals have been the subject of an EU moratorium since 2013, this means imidacloprid at least can hang around in the environment for years, still causing harm to bees.

The chemical companies may now be regretting shelling out £2.7 million for the study, although Bayer are probably regretting it more, since the evidence suggests that imidacloprid and clothianidin, both made by Bayer, are more harmful than thiamethoxam, made by Syngenta. In fact Syngenta have welcomed the study as 'a helpful contribution to the ongoing debate about pollinator health'. Bayer, on the other hand, have set about rubbishing the study, claiming it doesn't show what the published paper says it does (but trust me, it does).

In the debate that led to the current EU moratorium, the British government tended to side with the chemical companies, but was eventually overruled. Following Brexit, it will be interesting to see if part of taking back control means regaining the freedom to continue poisoning our bees. This study should help to make sure it does not.

Hello again, crab spider

Move from Sheffield to Devon, as I did recently, and everything changes: rainfall, temperature and soil to mention only the most obvious. It may even be worth having another go with plants that I tried in Sheffield, and that turned out to be the horticultural equivalent of banging your head against a brick wall (*Tropaeolum speciosum* springs to mind). But one of the less apparent changes is the opportunity to renew my acquaintance with one of the garden's more charismatic (but mostly overlooked) inhabitants: *Misumena vatia*, the common flower crab spider.

Crab spiders have found a way of finding and catching prey that is so neat, and at the same time so obvious, that you wonder why more spiders don't do it. Many different kinds of spiders use silk to create a huge variety of sticky traps, snares and tripwires, some chase down their prey, and others have evolved remarkable jumping ability. But crab spiders do none of these things; they simply sit in flowers and wait for their food to come to them.

Which would be interesting enough, but *Misumena* has another interesting ability (I'm almost tempted to call it a 'superpower'): it's able to change colour. Not almost instantly, like a chameleon or a cuttlefish, but over a few days. Crab spiders' default colour is white or cream, but they can change to almost any shade of yellow, and then back to white again. The matching against a yellow flower background can be quite uncanny, rendering the spider all but invisible, at least to human eyes.

There has been a lot of argument about exactly why crab spiders do this. The first explanation likely to occur to you is that the spider is hiding from the bees, flies and butterflies it is hoping to catch. But spiders of all kinds are also a favourite food of birds, so maybe they are hiding from their own predators. Some fancy research, simulating how crab spiders might appear to both birds and bees, has left the question unresolved; they could be hiding from either – or both. But a complication is that they often don't seem to be trying very hard. That is, if you collect crab spiders from a range of white and yellow flowers, they don't seem to match where you collected them much better than by chance.

Fortunately, other observations can help us to discover what crab spiders are up to. One large study of the stomach contents of birds found the remains of over 10,000 spiders, of which just four were *Misumena*. So birds eat very few crab spiders. Of course, that could just mean that the crab spider's camouflage is perfect. But no camouflage is that good, and you would expect birds to detect spiders moving between flowers, or while they were eating their (much more conspicuous) prey. Moreover, one researcher spent 30 years studying crab spiders without witnessing a single bird attack. So it looks like birds don't bother with crab spiders, but we don't know why not.

At the same time, other researchers have been studying how well potential prey can detect crab spiders. Crab spiders are quite small, so they are more dangerous for smaller bee species. One study found that small bees tended to avoid patches of flowers with crab spiders, and to prefer spider-free patches. But how do the bees know the spiders are there? The answer is they don't. Bees rapidly left flower patches infested with spiders, but only after experiencing a 'close call' (i.e. surviving an unsuccessful attack). So it looks like bees are unaware of crab spiders until they are attacked. Which all suggests that whatever else it may do, the crab spider's camouflage is certainly very good at fooling insect pollinators.

Crab spiders are found only south of a line from North Wales to Lincolnshire, and are only really common in the south-east and in southern coastal counties. There definitely weren't any in Sheffield, so it's nice to have them back.

Daylight robbery

Around ten years ago, I bought a plant of blackcurrant sage, *Salvia microphylla*. A native of Mexico and the southern USA, blackcurrant sage was not reliably hardy in my old garden in Sheffield, so it lived in a big pot that went in a cold greenhouse in the winter. Like several similar New World sages with red flowers, blackcurrant sage is pollinated by hummingbirds. So, not surprisingly, its flowers are not really designed with bees in mind, unlike culinary sage, *Salvia officinalis*, which is a favourite plant with bees in my garden.

Culinary sage has a nice open flower, with plenty of room for a bee to get its head inside in search of nectar. But blackcurrant sage flowers are laterally flattened, so any would-be pollinator needs a tongue long enough to reach the nectar from outside, which most bees don't have. However, I soon noticed that bumblebees were getting round this in the way they often do, by simply biting a hole near the base of the flower. The culprit is almost certainly *Bombus terrestris*, the buff-tailed bumblebee, an insect that is such a hardened criminal that I swear it sometimes 'robs' flowers that would be easier to access via the 'official' route. Once you start to look, you realise how rare it is to see a comfrey or aquilegia flower that *hasn't* been robbed by *Bombus terrestris*.

Research has shown that bumblebees learn to bite holes in flowers to get at the nectar by watching other bees. But in the case of blackcurrant sage there's an extra complication. The flowers have distinct left and right sides, and in my plant all had been robbed on the right side. It makes sense if flowers are all robbed on the same side; bees are normally exploiting existing holes, rather than making new ones, so it saves time if they know which side of the flower to go to.

But why the *right*? Maybe most bees, like most people, are right handed? Or maybe the first bee to make a hole chooses a side at random, and all subsequent robbers just follow that cue? Or perhaps (less likely, but still possible), the queen bumblebee comes out of hibernation in the spring remembering which side was robbed the previous year, and carries on with the same side? Nothing for it but to investigate.

I started with the patch of salvias in the Botanical Gardens in Sheffield. Sure enough, most flowers were robbed, and all on the same side – the right. The following summer, my plant wasn't robbed at all, but the Botanical Garden salvias were, once again, all robbed on the right. That summer I visited Kew, and headed for the long border by the rock garden, on the opposite side from the Princess of Wales Conservatory, which is full of salvias. As I confidently approached the Kew salvias, I was already mentally composing my Nobel Prize acceptance speech for the discovery that bumblebees are right handed.

As I expected, the Kew salvias were nearly all robbed, and all on the same side too – the left side. In fact, since then, it's become clear that although the salvias in any one spot are always robbed on one side only, it's not always the right, and nor is it always the same as last year. Over six years the Sheffield sequence was RLLLRR, and at Kew LRRRLL. In other words, just the sort of sequences you would expect from tossing a coin.

I no longer have occasion to visit Kew every year, so that line of enquiry is closed. I've also moved away from Sheffield, but I did bring the salvia with me, so I look forward to seeing if Devon bees are as given to thievery as their Yorkshire cousins.*

Overlooked pollinators

When gardeners think about pollinators, we usually think first about bees. Nothing surprising about that; bees are extremely abundant in gardens, and normally the most important pollinators. After bees, we tend to move on to

---

* They are.

butterflies – not the most significant pollinators by a long way, but both conspicuous and attractive.

Which all rather leaves hoverflies in the shade, and that's a pity. Because from a gardening perspective, hoverflies are the ultimate win-win insects: the adults are abundant, attractive, harmless and valuable pollinators, while the larvae of many of the commonest garden species are huge consumers of aphids. In short, there's plenty to like about hoverflies, and little or nothing to dislike (once you've figured out how to tell them apart from wasps, that is). But although most gardeners are aware that it pays to keep pollinators happy, advice specifically about hoverflies is rather thin on the ground.

One thing that's well known about hoverflies is they have short tongues, compared to bees and butterflies, and this limits the flowers from which they can extract nectar. But which flowers exactly? This is the question a Dutch team asked recently, in research published in the *Journal of Applied Ecology*. Rather than just observing which flowers hoverflies like to visit, they took the unusual step of conducting experiments that measured exactly how well hoverflies were able to survive on different flowers. Control hoverflies given plain water died after only a couple of days, while those given a sugar solution survived much longer. Their test animal was the marmalade fly *Episyrphus balteatus*, frequently the commonest hoverfly in gardens.

Their results were conclusive, and slightly surprising. Only very shallow flowers (less than 2mm deep) were any use at all to the marmalade fly; if the flowers were any deeper, the flies didn't survive any longer than on pure water. Among the members of the daisy family the critical depth was even less, around 1mm, possibly because the very narrow, tightly packed florets make access difficult. Other parts of their study confirmed this crucial 1–2mm depth; for example, in strips of sown wildflowers in the field, hoverfly abundance was directly correlated with the proportion of these very shallow flowers.

What does this mean in practice? Well, it certainly confirms the pre-eminence of the very shallow flowers of the carrot family as nectar sources for hoverflies. All the umbellifers tested, including carrot itself, along with parsnip, coriander, fennel, hogweed and *Ammi majus*, were excellent for hoverflies. As were several other shallow flowers with easily-accessible nectar: buckwheat, borage, gypsophila and yarrow.

On the other hand, some very good 'bee plants' were hopeless, for example *Phacelia tanacetifolia*. And from the marmalade fly's perspective, the excellent bee flowers *Cosmos* and *Calendula* were no better than water; both have flowers much deeper than the 2mm threshold. There were some surprises too: cornflower and sunflower both turned out to be good, despite having relatively deep flowers. But both have 'extrafloral nectaries', i.e. they produce nectar *outside* the flowers.

Finally, if you value your hoverflies, please don't forget their larvae – unattractive (basically maggots), but definitely on your side in the war against aphids. Before you squash the greenfly on your roses, or blast them with the hose, check first that they aren't already being hoovered up by hoverfly larvae. They probably are.

Shedding light on the decline of moths

Spare a thought for moths. There are around 800 species of large moths in the UK, and about 1,600 species of smaller so-called 'micro-moths'. Both adult moths and their cater-pillars are important food for bats, birds and a great deal of other garden wildlife, and they're also useful pollinators, albeit mostly at night, when their activities remain unob-served. Despite all this, moths get only a tiny share of the attention devoted to our 50 or so species of butterflies.

All the evidence also shows that moths are in serious long-term decline. They are hardly unusual in that, and the causes are no doubt at least partly the usual suspects: cli-mate change, habitat loss and fragmentation, pollution and eutrophication. But for moths these horsemen of the apoca- lypse are joined by another: everyone who has noted the decline of moths has suggested that increased night-time lighting must have something to do with it. It's easy to show experimentally that artificial lighting can increase mortality and reduce foraging and reproduction of individual moth species; yet no one has so far managed to pin any part of the general decline of moths on light pollution.

Recently, Dutch researchers set out to find the smok- ing gun (if there is one), and their results were published in the journal *Global Change Biology*. They exploited the fact that although most moths are nocturnal, some are not. And similarly that although most moths are attracted to artificial light, some are not. Clearly, if artificial light is a major cause of decline in moths, those that fly during the day, or that are indifferent to light, should be declining less, if at all.

A database of over 3.5 million records of Dutch moths allowed the researchers to calculate the population trend for 481 species of large moths over the period 1985–2015. Given the traditionally messy nature of ecological results, their findings were surprisingly clear: day-flying moths, and those unattracted to light, had scarcely declined at all over the last three decades. In contrast nocturnal moths, and those attracted to light, showed severe declines.

These results provide strong support for what many had long suspected: increased lighting, caused by expanding urbanisation and more, better-lit, roads has been a major cause of the decline of our moths. Indeed studies of a handful of species have shown that artificial light is now such a powerful selective force that a few moths have begun to evolve to become less sensitive to light.

Much of this, of course, is outside the control of gardeners. Better design of street lighting, with dimmer, better shielded, longer wavelength lights (less attractive to moths) that are lit only when and where they're really essential, would help a lot. But at least street lighting is genuinely useful, making roads safer for both motorists and pedestrians. The same cannot be said of most garden lighting. Even if you love your garden so much that you'd like to be able to admire it at any hour of the day or night, think of the local wildlife before you buy those must-have outdoor lights.

Running shoes for bugs

Suddenly, and rather surprisingly, the humble froghopper is front-page news, as a possible future vector of the deadly bacterial plant disease *Xylella fastidiosa*, should it ever arrive in Britain. So gardeners are being asked to report sightings of the bugs, or more specifically the blobs of froth

31

that young froghopper nymphs blow out of their backsides, and then hide in while feeding on plant xylem fluid – the familiar 'cuckoo spit'.

But there's more to froghoppers than cuckoo spit; as adults, froghoppers are capable of some of the fastest and most powerful jumps (for their size) in the animal kingdom – far outperforming real frogs. Acceleration from a standing start to a take-off velocity of almost 5 metres per second can last less than a millisecond, exposing the froghopper to 550 g, a force that would squash me or you flat as a pancake. How that acceleration is achieved is an interesting story in itself, but here I want to consider a different problem: how to take off without slipping. The story was revealed recently in research reported in the journal *Proceedings of the National Academy of Sciences*.

When froghoppers jump, they don't want to just go straight up in the air, they want to actually get somewhere, so although jump angle varies, it averages somewhere around 45°. The result is powerful horizontal forces on whatever they happen to be standing on, which could easily cause their feet to slip. Indeed, when researchers persuaded froghoppers to jump from a sheet of glass, they did slip, and the resulting jump was rubbish: low speed, high angle and usually uncontrolled spin too.

Faced with the same problem, human sprinters came up with spiked running shoes, and froghoppers have done exactly the same. Their hind legs are equipped with arc-shaped rows of sharp, backward-facing spines. Nor does the resemblance end there. Spikes on running shoes have a lot to put up with, so of course they're metal, or sometimes ceramic. Froghoppers' spines need to be tough too, so they're tipped with zinc. This is a common strategy among insects; mouthparts and ovipositors that pierce or cut plant tissue are often reinforced with zinc or manganese. Even so, the researchers found that the spines often had broken tips, one reason why froghoppers seem to have more spines than they really need, presumably to allow for such damage.

Spikes on running shoes provide traction by penetrating the running surface, and froghopper spines do the same. After a froghopper had taken off from a leaf, electron microscopy revealed they leave tiny holes in the leaf, each about 10–15 millionths of a metre across.

Any insect that wants to jump from a smooth surface like a leaf faces the problem of slipping, but the 'spiked running shoe' option is not the only one adopted by jumping insects. Leafhoppers, although closely related to froghoppers and also common in gardens, achieve the high friction forces required for a jump by having soft, pad-like structures on their hind legs, which contact the surface briefly during the acceleration phase of the jump. So leafhoppers *can* take off from a sheet of glass, and they can also transmit plant diseases, but don't produce cuckoo spit.

Getting up close to creepy-crawlies

A gift-shop staple is the 'bug viewer', a clear plastic container with a magnifying lid, designed to allow you to examine an insect or other creepy-crawly that you may have encountered in your garden. They're usually packaged to attract children, but adults seem to have just as much fun with them. The instructions are typically very simple: 'Capture your creepy-crawly, snap on the magnifying lid and take a closer look.' But that does rather gloss over the most difficult part, rather like the apocryphal first line of the recipe for jugged hare: 'First catch your hare.'

In short, bug viewers are designed for viewing bugs, not for capturing them. The instrument for catching your bug, used by generations of entomologists but at the same time virtually unknown to the general public, is the pooter (unknown to my Word spellchecker too, which suggests 'pouter'). To the more literary among you, 'Pooter' will forever be the hero of George and Weedon Grossmith's Victorian classic *The Diary of a Nobody*. The *Diary* is one of the funniest and most enduringly influential of comic novels, and its hero Charles Pooter is clearly a direct ancestor of Adrian Mole. If you haven't read it, then it's time you did.

Googling 'pooter', to my slight surprise, mostly turns up a hand-held device intended to produce authentic farting noises; YouTube is awash with examples of it in action. All good honest fun (well, it made me laugh), but quite unrelated to the bug-catcher, which is 'A bottle for collecting small insects and other invertebrates, having one tube through which they are sucked into the bottle and another, protected by muslin or gauze, which is sucked.' In other words, a device that allows you to suck an insect off a leaf and into a bottle, while avoiding any possibility of the insect ending up in your mouth. I say 'any possibility' because pooters are moderately fool proof, but not completely so; Dave Goulson describes a classic pooter accident in his excellent book *A Sting in the Tale*.

The delightful name comes from the equally splendid name of its inventor, William Poos, an American entomologist who first described it in a paper in 1929. According to the *Dictionary of Entomology*, Poos employed it to collect and study Cicadellidae, or leafhoppers to you and me. Given how hard leafhoppers are to catch, one can see why he needed a pooter. Poos' original illustration looks exactly like one you might use today, with the elegant addition (somehow appropriately for the roaring twenties) of a cigarette holder as a mouthpiece.

It's possible to make your own pooter, but much easier to buy one. Amazon will sell you one (and a bug viewer too), although I assume the reviewer who says 'Absolute game changer. This pooter is top notch and is going to really sort out all the problems I have going on in my life' is being mildly ironic. But *the* place for entomological supplies (including a whole range of pooters) is Watkins & Doncaster (http://www.watdon.co.uk/), a family firm who have been supplying the needs of naturalists the world over for more than 140 years.

Many thanks to Simon Leather for enlightening me about the history of the pooter.

Making bees count

The finding that wasps are smart was big news recently – big enough news to find its way onto BBC comedy panel show *Have I Got News For You?* For those of you who weren't paying attention, wasps have been shown to possess 'transitive inference'; that is, if they know that A is bigger than B, and that B is bigger than C, they can infer that A must be bigger than C.

Bees cannot do this, which might lead you to the erroneous conclusion that bees are dumb. But far from it – evidence continues to accumulate that bees are far smarter than anyone thought. More than twenty years ago, German researchers showed that honeybees can count. Specifically, they can use the number of landmarks to measure the distance to some food; if the food was after, say, three artificial landmarks, and researchers moved the landmarks (and the food) closer, the bees knew the food was now closer. That is, they knew the food was after the third landmark, rather than at a specific distance.

Fast forward more than a decade, and again German researchers showed that honeybees can match two visual patterns (again to find food), using only the number of elements in the pattern. Bees trained to visit, say, two (rather than three) blue dots were then able to find food marked by two (rather than three) yellow lemons. What's more, bees trained to do this could then do exactly the same with *three* dots (or lemons or stars) without any extra training – they had not just learned a one-off party trick, they had grasped the *idea* of using counting to find food.

But, which is where it gets really interesting, bees struggled to do any of this once numbers were above three. Which places them approximately at the level of human infants, who can discriminate arrays containing one, two, or three objects, but fail with arrays greater than three. More generally, the number of items that humans can hold in their short-term memory, and subsequently recall, has been repeatedly shown to be about four. Which is entirely consistent with my personal experience; send me to the shops for four items and there is at least a chance I'll return with all of them. But five? No chance – that's what shopping lists are for.

Recently, still on the subject of using numerical patterns to find food, Australian researchers have trained bees to understand the idea of 'more than' and 'less than'. After such training, bees were then able to infer that 'nothing' is less than one, and thus comes at the bottom end of the sequence 4, 3, 2, 1 …. In short, bees have some understanding, if only a slightly fuzzy one, of the concept of zero.

Finally, in research published only this year, an Australian/French team have demonstrated 'symbolic representation of numerosity' in bees. That is, bees can match a number (three dots, say) to a picture (a letter N, say), or vice versa, although bees trained to do this in one direction can't then reverse the matching process. They can easily reverse non-numerical matching, say of a colour to a scent, so this looks like a specifically numerical limitation.

So we are finally learning the limits of numerical intelligence in bees, which stretch much further than we thought, considering that the honeybee brain is only about the size of a sesame seed. Surely it's only a matter of time before someone suggests extending 'human rights' to bees, except we'd then have to do the same for wasps, and I can't see that catching on.

Toxic Tilia?

Is the nectar of lime-tree flowers toxic for bees? Plenty of people seem to think so. In his super book *A Sting in the Tale*, Dave Goulson says: 'Buff-tailed and white-tailed bumblebees love the flowers of lime trees, although there is something in the nectar which seems to make them dopey and even sometimes to kill them.' Sometimes pollen gets the blame; in his book *Scent in Your Garden*, Stephen Lacey says: 'limes have extremely powerfully scented flowers, and they would be planted more often if … their pollen did not contain a narcotic element that stupefies bees'.

The lime most often claimed to have toxic nectar is the silver lime, *Tilia tomentosa*, about which the RHS website says: 'Clusters of highly scented yellowish flowers are narcotic to bees'. Although several limes are on the RHS 'perfect for pollinators' list, the silver lime is not, presumably on account of its alleged toxicity.

The belief that lime trees can harm bees has been around since at least the 16th century, so a couple of Kew botanists decided that it was time to review all the latest evidence. Their conclusions were published in the journal *Biology Letters*.

Over 50 years ago it was suggested that the sugar mannose, which is toxic to bees, was present in lime nectar, and this is still frequently cited as the problem. But recent analyses show that lime nectar does not contain mannose. In fact the whole idea that there might be anything toxic in lime nectar is hard to sustain; if comatose bees found under lime trees are fed lime nectar, they quickly recover and fly away. So lime trees are not like, for example, *Rhododendron ponticum*, whose nectar really is toxic, at least to honeybees (but not to bumblebees).

What are the other possibilities? Very occasionally, bees may be killed by a lime tree that has been sprayed with insecticides to control aphids. Predation is another possibility; in his book Dave Goulson reports dead bees under lime trees that had been killed by great tits. But most of the time the dead or dying bees found under lime trees are uninjured, so there must be some other cause. Which really only leaves us with starvation. Towards the end of the flowering season, lime flowers secrete little nectar, but bees continue to visit. Bees have been recorded returning 'empty' from visiting lime trees, and dying bees found below lime trees have very low energy reserves. The starvation hypothesis would also explain why the dead bees found under lime trees are usually bumblebees rather than honeybees, since the latter have access to honey stores back at the hive.

But why do bees continue to visit lime flowers when

there is little or no nectar? Lime flowers emit the same volatile compounds that bumblebees use to recruit workers to a good food source. But these chemicals are commonly produced by many other flowering plants, so although they may have evolved by plants to attract pollinators, this is far from unique to *Tilia*. But lime nectar also contains caffeine, and recent research has shown that caffeine-laced nectar persuades bees to return to the same flowers, even if they now offer little real reward.

The relationship between bees and flowers may look like one of benign cooperation, but in reality each side is constantly striving to get more than its fair share from the bargain. Using caffeine to trick bees into continuing to visit empty flowers may just be one of the weapons in this long-running struggle.

Plant more flowers

The recent confirmation of a permanent ban on neonicotinoid insecticides is welcome news, but pollinators are not out of the woods yet. There's no shortage of advice on what gardeners can do to help, most of it focused, understandably enough, on what sort of plants we should be growing. Or, to put it another way, on the *quality* of the resources that gardens provide for pollinators.

But, as more than one exasperated bee must have thought, confronted by yet another post-modern wasteland of grasses, bamboos, tree ferns and tastefully-arranged rocks: never mind the quality, what about the width? It's all very well growing the right plants, but are we growing enough? And how many is enough anyway? In attempting to answer that question, I focus on bees, for two reasons. First, they're nearly always the most important pollinators. And second, of all the common pollinators, they depend most completely on flowers. I also focus specifically on pollen, rather than nectar, because although bees need both, pollen is a vital protein-rich food for raising young bees. And since flowers respond to nectar consumption by producing more, nectar is to some extent a renewable resource, but pollen definitely isn't; when a flower opens, it contains a fixed amount of pollen, and when it's gone, it's gone.

So let me re-phrase that question: how much pollen do bees need, and what does that mean in terms of flower numbers? Those who had the job of devising the measures targeted at pollinators in the Defra Countryside Stewardship scheme asked themselves exactly the same question, and quickly realised that a lot of educated guesswork would be needed to arrive at any kind of answer. For most bees we don't know how many colonies or nests there are per unit area of garden or countryside, or how much pollen is needed for each bee larva, and for most plants we don't know how much pollen there is per flower. Nevertheless, a team led by Lynn Dicks from Cambridge University did their best, and their deliberations are reported in a recent paper in the journal *Ecological Entomology*.

Their main conclusion is that rearing young bees takes an awful lot of pollen, and thus an equally large number of flowers. Earlier Swiss work had already shown that it takes the pollen from tens or even hundreds of flowers to raise a single (small) solitary bee larva. New data for British wildflowers and (much larger) bumblebees suggest that the Countryside Stewardship requirement of 2 hectares of flower-rich habitat per 100 hectares of farmland is enough – just – only if you make the most optimistic assumptions. Make some more pessimistic – some would say realistic – assumptions about pollen supply and demand, and there's no way any feasible scheme could even begin to supply the quantities of pollen required.

The inevitable conclusion, that intensive farmland doesn't even come close to supplying the needs of bees, makes sense of other research on bees. Bigger bees need more pollen, and although it's well-known that all bees have tended to decline recently, larger bees have suffered more than small ones. New research from the Netherlands shows an even more interesting result; over the last 150 years, large bees have become measurably smaller, almost certainly because smaller bees can make do with less food; small bees haven't changed in size. Compare that with Dutch citizens, who have become 10% *taller* over the same period, largely as a result of improved nutrition (mostly from intensive farming; our gain is the bees' loss).

The message for gardeners is a simple one: while growing the right flowers is important, it's at least as imperative to grow lots of them. You can't have too many flowers, especially in March and April, when queen bumblebees are waking up and establishing new colonies. You already grow pulmonarias? Good – now grow a few more.

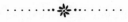

Flowers for bees

'All the flowers in the field were made to please the bees'. Or at least, so said that great 20th-century philosopher Freddie Garrity, in Freddie and the Dreamers' 1963 hit 'You Were Made For Me'. Freddie's opinion certainly matches most bees' view of the world. The flowers might agree too – up to a point.

The problem is that flowers and bees have a difference of opinion about what pollen is actually *for*. Plants are clear on this: pollen is the male gametes, the conduit for male genetic information, and nothing is more important than getting it safely from the anther of one flower to the stigma of another. For bees, on the other hand, pollen is a convenient, portable, high-protein food source, essential for feeding to larval bees.

So pollen is essential for both bees and plants to raise the next generation. To understand why a conflict arises, we have to understand how bees collect pollen. Bees use their forelegs and mandibles to strip pollen from the anthers, and then transfer it to special storage structures on the hindlegs or the abdomen; pollen groomed from the rest of the body also ends up here. Often mixed with nectar and saliva, this pollen load is sticky and quite unlikely to be brushed off on a stigma. Given the chance, bees can easily harvest all (or nearly all) the pollen from a flower, leaving none for pollination.

For the flowers, this is bad news. They don't mind sharing their pollen with bees, but they want some of it to end up somewhere on the bee's body that is safe from being groomed, and where it's likely to brush off on the stigma of the next flower visited; in short, at least some pollen needs to be protected from being simply taken away and eaten. Flowers have evolved two ways of doing this: offering nectar to divert the interest of bees away from pollen, and hiding the pollen so that it's difficult to collect, but likely to end up somewhere where the bee doesn't immediately notice it.

This second option has led to the evolution of the classic two-lipped 'bee flower'. Such flowers have a lower lip, or 'floor', where the bee lands. Anthers and stigma are under an upper lip, or 'roof'; as a bee pushes into the flower to get to the nectar, pollen is deposited on the bee's back, then brushed off on the stigma of the next flower entered.

The basic design both makes the pollen hard to collect, and applies it to the bee where it can't easily remove it, and where it often isn't easily noticed. This type of flower has evolved separately on many occasions, and occurs in tens of thousands of species, many of them familiar to gardeners; examples include *Acanthus*, *Roscoea*, *Canna*, *Digitalis*, horse chestnut, *Paulownia*, *Impatiens*, *Lobelia*, *Linaria* and *Abelia*. Some whole families, such as the mint and orchid families, are characterised by two-lipped flowers. In fact, this flower shape is a reasonable guide – though not a perfect one – to a good 'bee-flower'.

Variations on the basic design are numerous. To give bees something else to worry about, and make them even less likely to notice the surreptitious deposition of pollen on their backs, some flowers have partly closed the entrance, meaning the bee has to force its way in. The obstruction can be formed from the roof (e.g. *Iris* and *Phlomis*) or the floor (e.g. *Nemesia*). A particularly interesting variation is found in many species of *Salvia*. Here there are two stamens, but only one anther of each is fertile, and this fertile anther is situated high above the floor, much too high to contact the back of a visiting bee. The second anther is sterile, and the tissue that connects the two extends downwards into an arm that more or less closes the entrance to the flower. Thus the two anthers form a lever mechanism; as the bee pushes against the lower sterile anther, the whole arrangement pivots and presses the fertile anther onto its back. As the bee backs out of the flower, everything returns to its original position.

Two-lipped flowers look like the flowering plants' best option for using bees to transport their pollen, while at the same time preventing them from stealing all of it. But there's nothing to stop either partner cheating, and what looks like a harmonious partnership is more like an arms race with each side constantly trying get more than its fair share out of the arrangement.

Ecology at Chelsea 2016

The British Ecological Society (BES), the world's oldest ecological society, was 100 years old in 2013. So was the Chelsea Flower Show, so it seemed a natural part of the BES's centenary celebrations to stage an exhibit – for the first time – in the Discovery Zone at Chelsea. This was such fun that the BES came back for more in 2015, and is back again this year.

The theme this year is pollinators, and the exhibit focuses on the often-overlooked fact that the flowers we love to grow in our gardens evolved for the sole purpose of attracting a wide range of animal pollinators, from bees to birds, and from bats to lizards. So, however much *we* may like them, flowers can only really be understood if you know which animals they evolved to attract.

Many of our familiar garden flowers evolved to attract bees and butterflies, and we're lucky that bees and butterflies generally seem to like the same colours and scents that we do. If a majority of plants had evolved to attract flies that like to lay their eggs in rotting carrion (as some do), it's hard to imagine that humans would ever have taken up gardening in the first place.

Some pollinators are abundant in gardens, but normally escape attention because they work at night. So even though we have only about 50 species of butterflies in Britain, but around 800 species of large moths, it's the former that get most of the attention from gardeners. Moths like many of the same flowers as butterflies, but flowers that really specialise on moths have a characteristic syndrome: a deep flower tube, pale colour and strong scent, especially at night – all geared to pollinators that have long tongues and rely more on scent than sight. Some of our favourite scented garden plants, such as jasmine and nicotiana, evolved to attract moths.

All our native bats are insect eaters, but in the tropics thousands of species of plants are routinely pollinated by bats. Bat flowers tend to be strongly scented too, since they're also trying to attract a nocturnal pollinator, but opinion is divided on the appeal of the scent to a human nose. We now know that the scents of bat flowers often contain sulphur compounds, which can seem a bit cabbage-like to humans. Fortunately we don't need to worry too much about the smell of bat flowers, since hardly any are hardy enough to grow outdoors in Britain. Agaves, with flowers sometimes described as smelling like fermenting or rotting fruit, are one of the few exceptions.

Something else we lack in Britain is native plants adapted to bird pollination. I always envy American gardeners their hummingbirds, but there are bird-pollinated flowers in many other parts of the world, e.g. South Africa. Birds that pollinate flowers have highly specialised beaks and tongues to help them feed on nectar from deep, tubular flowers, which are often yellow, red or orange and usually unscented. We used to think bird flowers were unscented because birds don't have much of a sense of smell, but the lack of scent may be an attempt by bird flowers to avoid competition from bees. Among garden plants, it's interesting to contrast our native honeysuckle, a classic moth flower (pale, scented), with the north American trumpet honeysuckle (*Lonicera sempervirens*), a classic hummingbird plant (red, unscented).

The BES exists to support and promote ecological research, so one of the features of the exhibit will be cutting-edge research on floral yeasts. Research at Stanford University in the USA is investigating the role that yeasts in the genus *Metschnikowia* play in pollination. This yeast emits volatile organic compounds that mimic the floral scents of flowers, thus attracting more pollinators and increasing the reproductive success of both the yeast and the plant that hosts it. If you're coming to Chelsea, stop by the BES exhibit to have a sniff and see what you think.

Almost the last word on native and alien plants

If you want to attract native wildlife to your garden, do you need to grow native plants? That's the question the Royal Horticultural Society's Plants for Bugs project set out to answer nearly ten years ago. The project grew beds filled with plants of three declining levels of 'nativeness' (genuine natives, northern hemisphere 'near natives', and southern hemisphere 'exotics'), and then captured, identified and counted the invertebrates that turned up. Because the project produced such a vast mountain of data, the results are being analysed and reported in stages. The first report, nearly two years ago, concluded that as far as pollinators are concerned, it doesn't matter a great deal whether you grow natives or not.

But now – the big one. A new paper, in the journal *Biodiversity and Conservation*, reports the results of all the animals hoovered up by a 'Vortis' suction sampler: beetles, flies, bugs, spiders, springtails and wasps (parasitic and predatory), among others. The spiders, wasps and some of the other insects eat each other, but many of the insects captured eat plants. And because many plant-eating insects are quite picky about their diet, it's among this group that you might expect to find the closest dependence on native plants – essentially, if the plant they eat isn't there, you're not likely to find them.

So, what did they find? Well, not surprisingly, not all those very different kinds of insects and spiders responded to the different kinds of plants in exactly the same way. As expected, some were quite indifferent to plant origin; spiders, for example, whether web-spinners or active hunters, couldn't care less where the plants that make up their habitat come from. Nor would you probably expect insects that eat dead plants (*detritivores* – mostly springtails) to care much about plant origin, but they did – a little. This group, which made up nearly half the animals caught, was most abundant on native plants, but the exotics were only a little behind, with near-natives third.

But a very consistent picture emerged from most of the insect groups: natives were best, followed by near-natives and exotics in that order. On the other hand, the difference between the different kinds of plants was not large – plenty of wildlife was supported by all three. The other consistent message, whatever the origin of the plants, was that more is better: the bigger the volume of vegetation, the more insects of nearly every kind, a result that has also been shown by other research on garden wildlife. We can even put these two observations together to compare the relative importance of plant quality and quantity: to obtain the same number of insects as from a plot of native plants, you would need about a fifth more near-native vegetation, and about a quarter more exotic greenery.

Rather pleasingly, I think these findings will generally leave everyone feeling reasonably satisfied. Those who have always maintained that native is best will feel suitably vindicated. And since research has shown that the typical domestic garden is dominated by natives and near-natives, the take-home message for the gardener with wildlife in mind is to carry on as usual, but to concentrate on growing as much as possible, irrespective of where it comes from. As I've pointed out before, *how* you garden is at least as important as exactly *what* you grow.

Pesticides in garden plants

More and more of us like to garden in a way that encourages and benefits wildlife. Not surprisingly, the focus of much of this effort is pollinators – after birds, probably the most conspicuous and attractive garden wildlife. And when it comes to pollinators, even those of us who don't take a particular interest in wildlife are generally aware of the rules: grow the right kinds of plants, and try to avoid pesticides, but if you must use them, don't spray plants in flower, and don't use systemic insecticides at all on plants visited by bees.

But what if taking these reasonable precautions to avoid exposing pollinators to pesticides is a waste of time? What if the pesticides are already there, inside the plants, before you even buy them? To find out, Dave Goulson and colleagues from the universities of Sussex and Padua sampled leaves of 29 pollinator-friendly plants purchased from five retailers in East Sussex. The leaves, and pollen from eighteen of the plants, were analysed for the presence of a range of insecticides and fungicides, and the results published in the journal *Environmental Pollution*.

Plants from all five retailers contained pesticide residues, and only two of the 29 plants did not contain any of the pesticides tested. Most plants contained more than one pesticide; *Ageratum houstonianum* contained seven and *Erica carnea* contained ten different insecticides and fungicides. Not surprisingly, given their widespread use and long persistence inside plants, neonicotinoid insecticides were detected in more than 70% of the analysed plants, and pollen was contaminated with neonicotinoids at similar concentrations to leaves. What's more, the concentrations of neonicotinoids were similar to those found in treated agricultural crops, concentrations that have been shown in other research to have harmful effects on bees. Other contact poisons, such as chlorpyrifos and pyrethroids, were found in fewer plants, but sometimes at high concentrations.

It's impossible to say how much harm these plants might do to the pollinators in your garden. A few of them, among large numbers of uncontaminated plants, would probably do no harm at all. But if you planted up a whole bed with contaminated plants in spring, they might deliver a big dose of pesticides at a critical time in the growth of new bumblebee nests.

The good news is that Aldi, one of the retailers involved,

says it stopped using neonicotinoids in October 2016 (the plants tested were bought in July 2016). And B&Q has announced it will not allow its suppliers to use neonicotinoids from February 2018. But that still leaves a few other unpleasant chemicals, so the safest option is perhaps to buy your plants from a nursery that you know doesn't use pesticides at all, grow your own plants from seed or cuttings, or swap them with like-minded gardening friends.

The RHS 'Plants for Pollinators' logo remains one of the best guides to the right kinds of plants to grow for pollinators. Of course, the RHS has no control over how retailers actually grow the plants they recommend; nevertheless, in the light of this research, they are reviewing the scheme in case they need to make any changes to make sure they continue to provide the best possible advice.*

An interesting postscript is that Goulson's study, very unusually, was funded via the crowdfunding organisation Walacea. Maybe it's getting harder to fund important research like this through the usual channels; I wonder why that might be?

---

* One outcome of that review was a change of name, from 'Perfect for Pollinators' to 'Plants for Pollinators'.

A balanced diet is the bee's knees

Bees rank highly in the affections of gardeners, right up there with birds, butterflies and hedgehogs. Bees are also unique among insects in their complete dependence on flowers – more or less everything needed to fuel adult bees and to grow new young bees comes from pollen and nectar. So, not surprisingly, the quantities and qualities of food for bees provided by different flowers have been the subject of exhaustive research. So much so that you could be forgiven for thinking that there's nothing left to discover on the subject.

But of course there is, as some Polish research, published in the journal *PLOS ONE*, demonstrates. The researchers began with the unarguable fact that young, growing honeybees, just like growing children, need a range of elements to make their bodies. Some, such as phosphorus, potassium and (especially) nitrogen are needed in large amounts. Others, such as copper, iron, zinc and magnesium are needed in much smaller amounts. For young bees, all these elements must come almost entirely from pollen; nectar is a great source of energy, but provides few other nutrients.

So, here's the question: how do the ratios of these elements in the pollen of different flowers compare with the ratios required to make bees? Or to put that another way, do some pollen types represent more of a balanced diet than others?

Our knowledge of the elemental concentrations of the pollen of different plants is very far from complete, and the little we do know is often based on a single study. Nevertheless, the answer to that question turns out to be a definite yes. The composition of the pollen of some plants is very unbalanced, for example sunflower pollen is very low in phosphorus. Clover, on the other hand, is almost perfectly balanced, and given that clover has long been known to provide protein-rich pollen, it looks like an even better bee food than we had previously thought. Other legumes that provide well-balanced pollen include gorse and broad bean.

But don't panic; it's not necessary to grow only plants with nutritionally-balanced pollen, any more than every mouthful of your food needs to represent a balanced diet. Bees aren't stupid, and they're perfectly capable of putting together a decent diet by mixing pollen from different plants, provided they're given plenty to choose from. Yet more reason, in case you needed one, to grow a wide range of different flowers, ideally throughout the whole season from spring to autumn.

A surprising postscript to this research is that *all* pollen, without exception, is short of sodium, so no amount of pollen mixing can provide enough. There's hardly any in nectar either, yet bees seem to manage to get hold of enough of this element, so it must be coming from somewhere else. Honeybees are known to drink seawater where it's available, and may even attempt to drink human tears and sweat. Failing that, the slightly unsavoury answer is that bees get sodium from 'dirty water' containing decomposing organic matter, and also from urine and even (urgh) poo.

Bird-brains understand speed limits

When we call someone a 'bird-brain', we're generally suggesting they're a bit dim. But is that entirely fair on birds? Some recent research seems to show birds are smarter than we think, or smarter than I thought anyway.

Like much of the best research, it clearly began by observing some ordinary, indeed quite boring, feature of the natural world and asking 'hold on – how does that work?' In this case, two biologists from Quebec were driving down a road in western France and noticed that birds in the road (or on the verge) flew away as their car approached. Well, so what? – we all know that. But how do they know *when* to fly away? Too late could be fatal, but too early is a waste of energy and foraging time.

58

The two researchers decided to do an experiment, by timing bird behaviour while driving down a range of roads at varying speeds, either at, above or below the legal limit for that road. Yes folks, this research did indeed involve breaking the law, so please don't try this at home. There's no mention of what they planned to say if they ran into the *gendarmerie*, but disobeying the speed limit was necessary because they saw that birds must be doing one of two quite different things: assessing the speed of every approaching vehicle and acting accordingly, or simply learning the prevailing speed limit and judging when to fly based on that.

The research, reported in the Royal Society journal *Biology Letters*, quickly revealed that the latter is true. Birds fly sooner when approached by cars on fast roads, but pay no attention at all to how fast any individual car is travelling. Of course, like all interesting findings, this raises further questions, such as *how* birds come to learn the speed limits of particular roads (I think we can assume they can't read road signs). One possibility is that urban roads, with low (50 kph) speed limits, simply look different from more rural, higher-limit roads. But the researchers found that birds clearly distinguish between fast (90 kph) and very fast (110 kph) roads, even though those kinds of roads usually look very similar. Maybe birds come to associate something else, such as traffic density or road noise, with a particular speed limit. However they do it, it looks like a sensible strategy, since birds have enough to worry about without trying to work out the speed of every approaching vehicle.

All this leads me to suggest a couple of other things to think about. If further research reveals *how* birds evaluate the riskiness of different roads, it might allow us to design roads that are safer for wildlife, and even (who knows?) for people. And last but not least, this looks like another reason, in case you needed one, to obey the speed limit; if the limit is 30, other road users – and not just the ones with feathers – aren't expecting you to be doing 50.

Twenty-first century fox

Have you had a good look at the foxes that visit your garden recently? Over the years, do you think they've been getting bigger? Or smaller? The trouble is, there are good reasons to expect both trends.

To explain why, let me first of all introduce you to Bergmann's rule, arguably the oldest rule in ecology, in fact predating the coining of the word 'ecology' by nearly twenty years. One of the few ecological rules that really is true more or less all the time, Bergmann's rule says that among groups of related warm-blooded animals, body size increases as you get further from the equator. The reason is surface-to-volume ratio, which means that larger animals find it easier to keep warm in cold climates, while small animals lose heat and thus stay cool more easily in hot ones.

So one effect of a warming climate should be that mammals and birds are getting smaller. And, from stone martens in Denmark to songbirds in Israel, that's what many studies have found.

But there's another powerful force acting in exactly the opposite direction. For the last two hundred years, and especially since the Second World War, we've got used to our children being taller, on average, than we are (and increasingly, fatter too). Improved nutrition is certainly one of the main causes. But not only do we eat more, we also waste more, so maybe we would also expect the animals that share our towns and gardens – and eat our rubbish – to be getting bigger, while those that don't should be getting smaller, or at least staying the same size.

One of the best studies on this whole question was published in the journal *Functional Ecology* some years ago. Researchers in Israel measured specimens, collected throughout the second half of the 20th century by the Zoological Museum of Tel Aviv University, of five large mammalian predators that commonly live in towns and cities: the striped hyena, wolf, golden jackal, fox and badger. They also looked at specimens of two animals that have not adapted to live in close proximity to humans – the caracal and the jungle cat.

The results were clear: over a 50-year period, the wolf, golden jackal, striped hyena and badger had all become significantly larger. Supporting the idea that greater availability of tasty human garbage is the most likely explanation, the two carnivores that don't live close to humans showed no sign of any change in size over the same period. Over the period covered by the study, the human population of Israel increased nearly eight-fold and the standard of living tenfold, while numbers of livestock, total cultivated area and irrigated area also increased dramatically. All these changes mean more food for animals that are happy living near humans.

But the changes in size showed another interesting pattern; the bigger the animal, the greater the relative change in size. So the largest, the striped hyena, had increased most, while the second smallest, the badger, had changed least. And the smallest, the fox, hadn't changed at all. The explanation seems to be that size reflects the pecking order at preferred feeding sites, such as garbage dumps. Hyenas, if present, chase away the smaller carnivores, while the next largest, the wolf, is top dog as long as hyenas aren't around, and so on down the size hierarchy. The fox, at the bottom of the heap, is picked on by all the others and has to make do with the stuff nothing else wants to eat.

In Britain, of course, we lack all those larger carnivores, so our foxes can take their pick of our rubbish. Which suggests they ought to be getting bigger, but despite occasional reports of 'giant' foxes, there's no firm evidence that they are. I find it easy to imagine that the foxes in my garden get bigger every year, but maybe they're just getting cockier.

Do native plants taste better?

I've written about this subject before, but I make no apology for returning to it here, for it remains one of the chief conundrums for the dedicated wildlife gardener: the relative value of exotic and native plants for native wildlife. In some respects, this is clear enough. Pollinating insects are much the same the world over, so native bees and butterflies don't much care whether a plant is native or comes from Tierra del Fuego, as long as it has the right sort of flowers.

But it's when we consider the vast army of insect herbivores that the trouble starts. Moth and sawfly caterpillars, beetles and sap-sucking bugs are often relatively specialised in their feeding habits, eating only one kind of plant, or only a few closely-related species. Logic suggests that these insects will prefer to eat native plants, and they may refuse to eat foreign plants at all. In fact a whole branch of invasion biology is dedicated to investigating the Enemy Release Hypothesis (ERH), which says that alien plants do better, when moved to a new country, because they leave most of their specialist herbivores behind.

The ERH is a direct corollary of native insects preferring to eat native plants, but support is decidedly mixed, with most studies finding little or no evidence for it. Which brings me to a nice recent study, carried out in the Czech Republic by a team from Germany, Switzerland and the Czech Republic, and published in the *Journal of Ecology*. They looked at how much herbivory was experienced by nine pairs of plant species; each pair were in the same genus, but one was a Czech native and the other was an alien. For example, the native *Epilobium hirsutum* (great hairy willowherb) and the alien *E. ciliatum* (American willowherb).

Catching insect herbivores in the act isn't easy, as you'll know if you've ever tried. So they did what researchers often do in such circumstances, which is to look instead for evidence of their activity. They measured visible damage to leaves, stems and seeds, usually caused by caterpillars or molluscs, and the presence of herbivores that are easy to spot: leaf miners, stem borers and aphids. And because they were interested in anything that might give aliens an edge over natives, they also measured infection by mildew and rust fungi.

What did they find? In a word, nothing. Natives and aliens did not differ in the total amount of damage, or in the number of different *kinds* of damage (a very rough guide to the diversity of herbivores). Both are interesting results, but they're answering different questions, and total damage is probably the best predictor of the quantity of caterpillars, bugs and beetles, which is what matters to the birds, wasps, spiders and other predators that depend on them. In short, more damage equals more wildlife.

Interestingly, they did discover a big effect of soil fertility – irrespective of the identity of the species, or its native or alien status, plants on more fertile soils suffered more herbivory. Putting fertiliser on your plants doesn't just make them grow faster, it also makes them more tasty.

But the main finding, that native plants are no better for native herbivores than closely-related aliens, is good news for wildlife gardeners. For historical reasons, the entire temperate northern hemisphere shares a very similar flora, and the majority of British garden plants come from this flora; maples, oaks, birches, viburnums, roses, asters, primulas and a host of others are found right across

North America, Asia, Japan and mainland Europe – only the species differ. The result is that in the average British garden, half the exotic garden plants have native relatives in the same genus.

Of course, this means that many of your foreign garden plants will be quite attractive to native herbivores, which in turn means they will have quite a few holes in them. Even committed wildlife gardeners sometimes need reminding that this is supposed to be a good thing. If you don't want that to happen, go easy on the fertiliser, and grow plants that are as distantly related to our native flora as possible. Eucalyptus would be a good start.

Urban hedgehogs bounce back

All the evidence points to a big decline in hedgehog numbers over the last 50 years or so. The good news is that the decline in urban hedgehogs appears to have slowed, and there are even signs that they may be increasing in towns and cities. Since the main habitat used by hedgehogs in towns is private gardens, that means gardeners who want to help them (which is surely all of us) have a big responsibility.

So what makes a hedgehog-friendly garden? Before we can even start to answer that question, we need a reliable method of detecting hedgehogs. A team from Reading University set out to answer both questions, and their results were published in the journal *Urban Ecosystems*.

Hedgehogs were detected by issuing volunteer gardeners with footprint-tunnels, which use a food bait to lure animals across an ink pad so that their distinctive footprints are recorded on a removable sheet of paper. Over two years, they monitored over 200 back gardens in Reading, and found hedgehogs in about 32–40% of them (not all gardens were included in both years, and results for the two years were slightly different).

How good were gardeners at knowing whether they had hedgehogs in their gardens? The answer is not completely useless, but not very good either. In 13% of gardens hedgehogs were recorded where the owners hadn't noticed them, while in 22% of gardens they were not recorded where householders thought they were present. So gardeners were wrong about whether they had hedgehogs or not just over a third of the time. This wasn't exactly a surprise; in a previous study in Gloucestershire, also using footprint-tunnels, hedgehogs were recorded in 35% of gardens where householders had reported seeing them previously, but were also recorded in 38% of gardens where the householder had not reported seeing them.

So what makes a hedgehog-friendly garden? Unfortunately, this study failed to shed much light on that question. Although volunteers completed a questionnaire about garden features that might affect hedgehogs, including type of house (e.g. detached, terrace – strongly linked to garden size), presence of a pond, compost heap or log pile, use of slug pellets etc., none of these was related to hedgehog presence. The only thing that came close to significance was that hedgehogs were less likely to be found in gardens frequented by badgers; hardly surprising, since badgers are hedgehogs' only serious predator. In contrast, hedgehogs don't seem to care about either dogs or foxes.

One limitation of this study, and indeed any study that measures only hedgehog *presence*, is that hedgehogs travel long distances while foraging. So, although they might well stop long enough to hoover up the bait in a footprint-tunnel, they might only be passing through. Finding out where hedgehogs actually spend most of their time would mean fitting them with radio or GPS trackers, which has yet to be attempted with urban hedgehogs.

A final point is that although the volunteers in this study were selected independently of whether they thought they had hedgehogs or not, all the study gardens were at least potentially accessible to hedgehogs, via holes under fences, gates or gaps in boundaries. Inaccessible gardens weren't included at all, and the best – and simplest – thing you can do for hedgehogs is to make sure they can get in and out of your garden. Don't forget that even if your garden isn't your local hedgehogs' favourite, it might be blocking access to one that is. So if your garden is surrounded by a fence with no holes in, please go and make one, or more than one. In fact do that right now, before you forget.

NOT WORTH DOING, OR AT LEAST NOT WORTH WORRYING ABOUT

Homeopathy for gardeners

What is biodynamic gardening? Not a question I had given much thought to, until I chanced on a recent review of research into biodynamics, written by Linda Chalker-Scott, associate professor at Washington State University, and published in *HortTechnology*, a journal of the American Society for Horticultural Science. I've been a fan of Chalker-Scott ever since I read her book *The Informed Gardener*.

At the outset, Chalker-Scott emphasises that we mustn't make the common mistake of equating biodynamic gardening (or farming) with organic gardening. Many researchers seem to have made this mistake, or at least have compared biodynamic with conventional, non-organic practices. Since 'conventional' (non-biodynamic) organic gardening has powerful beneficial effects in its own right, this comparison makes it impossible to detect the extra effect, if any, due to biodynamics.

So what distinguishes biodynamic gardening from organic gardening? Not a lot; in fact biodynamic certification standards are nearly identical to those for organic farming. The only major difference is the use in biodynamic cultivation of special 'preparations' devised by Rudolf Steiner. To the average gardener, these preparations may seem a bit weird, consisting of things like cow manure packed into a cow's horn and chamomile flower heads fermented in soil. It's not clear how Steiner expected his preparations to work, or if he even checked whether they did. In fact Steiner, who was a philosopher, rejected scientific testing of his methods because he regarded them as self-evident or, as he said, 'true and correct unto themselves'.

Nevertheless, since biodynamic certification requires their use, most research has focused on whether Steiner's preparations do anything useful, and the short answer to that question is no. Whether looking at soil organic matter, microbial activity, pests and pathogens, or yield or chemical composition of crops, the overwhelming majority of studies have found no measurable differences between organic and biodynamic cultivation. Biodynamics has become popular among some wine makers, but one major study found no effect on grape quality or yield, while another found that tasters preferred the organic wine to the biodynamic product.

Chalker-Scott laments the shortage of research, and the often dubious quality of that which does exist. For example, one study looked at biodynamic preparations used in making compost, and reported a higher heap temperature and more nitrate in the finished compost. But in the same study numerous other variables were measured and all showed no effect. It's bad science to measure everything you can think of and then cherry-pick one or two isolated positive results, claiming they were what you were expecting all along. Statistics has routine methods to prevent exaggerated importance being attached to such exceptional results, but none of the authors who reported some effect of biodynamic preparations used them. In any case, another study found exactly the opposite effect of biodynamic preparations on compost heap temperature and nitrate concentration.

None of this should be very surprising. Biodynamic preparations are used in minute, homeopathic amounts, so all the usual arguments (and overwhelming evidence) against homeopathy apply here too. Nor does what they're supposed to do ('drawing in ordering forces from the cosmos') sound likely to me either, any more than why cosmic forces should be good for me or my garden; in fact, I think I'd rather stay out of the way of cosmic forces. And since biodynamic preparations must be kept away from 'the injurious influences of microwave radiation', it looks like you can't expect them to work anywhere you can get a mobile phone signal anyway. On the other hand, like homeopathy itself, they're very unlikely to do any harm, so if imagining you're in touch with cosmic forces sounds like your kind of thing, then go ahead.

What does biochar do?

It's taken me a while to get around to writing about biochar. The reason is simple: biochar research is a rapidly-moving target, with fresh results appearing all the time. But the arrival of yet another catalogue, attempting to sell me biochar and promising 'amazing results', has finally prodded me into action.

Let me say at the outset that biochar (basically charcoal) may do all kinds of things, but its effects on, say, soil microbes or heavy metals are huge research fields on their own. Here I focus on its effects on crop yield; first, because that's probably what gardeners are most interested in, and second, because those marketing biochar to gardeners clearly see better plant growth as its main selling point.

The recent pace of biochar research is astonishing; a study in 2011 that analysed all the existing research on biochar and crop yield found only sixteen studies, but by 2013, a new analysis found 103 studies. It's that 2013 analysis, conducted by researchers from China, Australia and Spain, and published in the journal *Plant and Soil*, that I rely on here. The authors conducted a formal meta-analysis, a statistical procedure that combines all the results from numerous independent studies.

First, the good news. Across all studies, biochar increased crop yield on average by about 11%, with some variation according to exactly how the experiment was conducted; in the field, the effect was a bit smaller, in pot studies it was a bit bigger. The effects lasted for at least two years, but in studies that lasted long enough to tell, there was no significant effect in the third or fourth years. And for the vegetable grower, more good news: the effects of biochar on vegetables tended to be larger than on grass or cereals.

The detail, as usual, reveals a complex picture. Biochar effects were *much* larger in sandy soils, and in those low in organic matter (which are often the same thing), than in loamy or carbon-rich soils. And there was an even bigger effect of pH: biochar had huge positive effects on acid soils, but none at all in soils around neutrality (pH 6.5–7.5). You can see why when you realise that biochar itself is very variable in pH, depending to a large extent on what it's made from, and at what temperature. Only biochar with a pH above 7 had positive effects on yield; *acid* biochar (pH below 7) had a significant *negative* effect on crop yield.

So what is biochar doing? As long as the biochar itself is alkaline, its primary effect is clearly liming. The results analysed in this study came from all over the world, and the most acid soils were from the tropics or subtropics, where soil acidity is often a major problem. The researchers conclude that biochar could be good for crops on acid tropical soils. On neutral soils, which is where your veg plot should be if you know what you are doing, biochar had no effect.

A secondary, but still large, effect is clearly on soil moisture; biochar helps to retain water on coarse, free-draining soils that would otherwise be at risk of suffering from drought. One sign of this is that several of the studies analysed looked at paddy rice, where water is not an issue and the effect of biochar was much smaller than in dryland crops. So a point worth making here (and one I've made before) is that one result of modern agriculture the world over tends to be soils that are low in organic matter, and thus poor at retaining moisture. Garden soils are usually much better in this respect, so it's not clear what extra moisture-retaining effect you could expect from biochar in a well-managed garden soil. Finally, it looks like there are a few plant nutrients in biochar too, but its fertiliser effect is small.*

There are probably enough studies on biochar now to draw some general conclusions. It looks like biochar improves the moisture-holding capacity of soils that are deficient in that respect, and often (but not always, depending on its pH) raises the pH of acid soils. Of course, gardeners have traditionally dealt with both those problems in other ways, by applying lime, making their own compost

* A more recent meta-analysis found that biochar made from nutrient-rich materials had a fertilising effect, but only in very low-nutrient tropical soils. In temperate agricultural (and garden) soils, which are usually fertile to start with, it didn't.

and sometimes by importing organic matter. All of which are highly effective, and probably cheaper than biochar.

Friends with benefits?

Using 'companion planting' to deter pests seems such a great, environmentally-friendly idea that we all – including me – really wish it could be shown to work. And in fact research has shown that growing cabbages with *anything* else can reduce egg-laying by cabbage root fly. The mechanism is complicated, but essentially flies looking for a cabbage to lay their eggs on are confused if they keep landing on something that isn't a cabbage.

The cabbage story does not involve the smell of the companion plant at all, which is why anything will do. But the idea persists that pests might be repelled by smelly companion plants – hence the excitement generated by recent research, published in *PLOS ONE*, showing that notoriously smelly French marigolds (*Tagetes patula*) can reduce the number of whiteflies on tomatoes. The research strongly suggests that the active ingredient of marigolds is limonene, found in citrus peel and widely used in everything from food to shampoo. Tomato plants grown with marigolds, or with an artificial source of limonene, had fewer whiteflies than when grown on their own.

All very encouraging, and yet it's tough to get companion planting to work in practice. *Which? Gardening* have tested companion planting on several occasions over the years, using a wide range of both crops and companions, and have never managed to make it work yet. Something always goes wrong: the intended pest fails to turn up, or the crop is clobbered by a different pest, or the companion is wiped out by pests, or – just about every time – competition from the companion plant itself reduces the yield of the crop.

So, even though the press release is optimistic (the findings might 'pave the way to developing safer and cheaper alternatives to pesticides'), I fear the latest research may prove to be a similar story. In the first place, it involves a greenhouse crop, which may well be essential if the repellent effect is to work properly; basically, out in the real world, the limonene may just blow away and never achieve the concentration necessary to bother the whiteflies. Not only that, there are other effective biological solutions for whiteflies in greenhouses, such as the parasitic wasp *Encarsia formosa*. We don't know how limonene might affect the wasp, or its interaction with whiteflies, but we do know that such complex systems are notoriously unpredictable.

I also have to report that marigolds did not increase the yield of tomatoes; indeed, tomato plants grown with marigolds, despite having fewer whiteflies, had slightly lower yields than plants grown on their own. The reason, as the researchers admit, was probably the same one that the *Which?* trials keep running into – the bushy marigold plants compete quite effectively with the tomatoes for light and space, especially when the latter are small, thus inhibiting their growth. And not only was the yield of each plant reduced, but there were only half as many tomato plants in the greenhouse when they were grown with marigolds, because half the pots that would otherwise contain tomatoes contained marigolds instead.

In short, to do better than a greenhouse full of tomatoes, marigolds would have to at least double the yield of each tomato plant, which they didn't come close to doing. But looking on the bright side, if you have plenty of space in your greenhouse and don't care too much about ending up with a few less tomatoes, marigolds are attractive and certainly won't do any harm.

Japanese knotweed myths examined

It 'chews through buildings, destroying walls and ripping up transport links', and 'tears through brickwork and concrete', according to one of many alarming newspaper reports. 'It', of course, is our old friend Japanese knotweed. Fortunately, some recent research has taken a close look at exactly what Japanese knotweed can and can't do, and the results, published in the journal *PeerJ*, may not be quite what you expected.

Contractors and surveyors were asked if they had experience of knotweed causing damage to residential buildings and, if so, how near the plant was to the damaged structure. Very few had, and in the few reported cases, the plant was touching the property or at most no more than 1m away. That distance is important, because banks will often refuse a mortgage (or impose conditions) where knotweed is within 7m of a building. The researchers went on to survey contractors with actual experience of excavating knotweed: the great majority found rhizomes only within 2.5m of the plant, and all except one within 4m.

Finally, the researchers conducted a case study of a genuine, worst-case scenario Japanese knotweed disaster area. Specifically, 68 residential properties in three streets in northern England, all built before 1900 and abandoned for at least ten years; all were in a state of disrepair, with cracked patios and crumbling brickwork. Naturally enough, all had also suffered from growth of plants, including knotweed, buddleja, ivy and miscellaneous trees and shrubs. Damage associated with these plants was surveyed, and compared with 'baseline damage' owing to neglect, weathering and wear and tear, regardless of plant presence.

The survey revealed that knotweed was only rarely associated with damage, and even when it was, it was evident that knotweed was an 'accessory after the fact', exploiting existing cracks or other damage. Moreover, knotweed was less damaging than other plants. The only example of a plant causing direct damage to a building was a falling tree; similarly, the only examples of a plant directly causing damage to walls were two walls being pushed over, one by buddleja, the other by a tree. Japanese knotweed never fell on anyone, and is incapable of pushing over a wall, never mind tearing, or even sneaking, through intact concrete or brickwork.

As the researchers conclude, knotweed's fearsome reputation is largely undeserved, other plants (native and alien) are worse, and the 7m rule is simply wrong. Nevertheless, I can believe you might still not like having knotweed around, so it's fortuitous that other research has recently looked at how best to kill it; results of the most thorough experimental study yet carried out were reported recently in the journal *Biological Invasions*.

The results were very clear: glyphosate is the best herbicide, and the best time to spray is from midsummer to autumn, at the time when the plant is busy moving resources (and therefore herbicide) from the leaves to the rhizome. Spraying was better than stem injection, cutting and spraying didn't improve on spraying alone, and nothing was achieved by using more than the recommended dose. Sadly for those not keen on herbicide, squashing the plant and covering with a light-proof membrane was the least effective treatment, but my guess is that covering, or just cutting down to the ground, would work *eventually*, as long as you were prepared to be thorough, patient and persistent.

But before you reach for the spray gun, I should complete our rundown of the latest knotweed research with the news that Japanese knotweed is a terrific late-season source of nectar for both bees and hoverflies. Nothing in life is ever as simple as it ought to be, is it?

The ifs and butts of garden bacteria

Just when you thought gardening was a relatively safe sort of hobby, along comes news of a hazard that probably hadn't even occurred to you. Researchers at Porton Down (and, as

I'm sure you're already thinking, no good news ever emerged from there, did it?) have been peering into the depths of your water butt. They were looking for *Legionella* bacteria, the organism that causes Legionnaires' disease.

First, the bad news: they looked at over 100 water butts and found *Legionella* in almost all of them. In most cases it wasn't possible to identify the exact species, but in a couple of cases *L. pneumophila* (the species that causes Legionnaires' disease) was positively identified. The less bad news is that they didn't find another species, *L. longbeachae*, which is commonly found in soil and compost and can also cause respiratory disease.

Now the good news. You catch Legionnaires' disease by breathing in tiny droplets of water containing *Legionella* bacteria, so not surprisingly the usual source is air conditioning systems, showers, hot tubs etc. It follows that people are normally infected in places like hotels, hospitals or offices where the bacteria have got into the water supply.

You're very unlikely to catch Legionnaires' disease at home and, despite the near-ubiquity of the bacteria in water butts, that's not going to change. The researchers investigated some normal watery gardening activities, starting with filling watering cans and then watering the garden. Some fancy sampling of the air within 1m of all this revealed no bacteria at all.

So a watering can is a completely useless way to

generate the bacterial aerosol that you need to breathe in to become infected. They then tried using a hose attached to a submersible water pump. This time they did manage to find the bacteria in the air, but only if the hose was used with a fine spray; a jet or coarse spray led to very few bacteria in the air.

So don't use a hose with a fine spray, which is a very inefficient way of watering the garden anyway, and your water butt will be pretty harmless. Indeed, as the authors of the study note, the risk of Legionnaires' disease while gardening 'is likely to be far outweighed by the benefits of exercise and outdoor activity'. On the other hand, normal hygiene good practice, such as always washing your hands after gardening, is definitely a good idea. And not particularly on account of *Legionella*; there are lots of unpleasant bacteria in soil that can make you ill if they get inside you.

One curious feature of their results concerns water temperature. The official advice is to keep water butts cool to prevent the growth of bacteria, but that didn't seem to be true. There was more *Legionella* in cooler water, and when the same butts were sampled in August and November, *Legionella* levels were higher in November. Given that the bacteria were in just about all the butts sampled, warm or cool, shady or sunny, and don't present much of threat anyway, I wouldn't go to any great trouble to try to keep your water butt cool.

A growing concern

Allotments have fertile, healthy soils, rich in organic matter, and support lots of wildlife. And both growing fresh fruit and veg and then eating them are good for you. So I think we can all agree that allotments are undiluted good news.

But – there's always a but – there is concern over the lead content of allotment soils, and indeed urban soils in general, especially in towns and cities with a long industrial history. Not to mention allotment-specific factors such as the occasional bonfire of lead-painted doors and window frames, and the widespread historic practice of using coal ash from domestic fires to improve the drainage of clay soils.

The upshot of all this is that many allotment soils are known to have lead levels well above the Environment Agency's safe level of 80mg per kilogram. This could be very bad news, so a consortium of researchers in Newcastle set out to try to discover how worried we should be. The results were published recently in the journal *Environment International*.

At three allotment sites in Newcastle, they first of all analysed the soil and, sure enough, 98% of samples exceeded the 80mg limit; a handful of samples were *ten times* over

86

the limit. But the blood of gardeners who worked the allotments was not unusually high in lead, indeed no higher than a random sample of their non-gardening neighbours. Lead in crops grown on the same allotments was also typically well below safe levels.

(The researchers were initially alarmed to find that one of their plotters had unusually high levels of lead in his blood. It turned out he'd been working on renovating some leaded windows; you can't be too careful with lead.)

So there's a lot of lead in allotment soil, but not much in the crops grown in that soil, or in the blood of the people who regularly eat those crops. What is going on? A clue is that there's no relationship between lead level in the soil of a particular allotment and in the crops harvested from that allotment; the total amount of lead in a patch of soil is no guide to lead in the crops grown in it.

In reality the 'safe' limit of 80mg is a worst-case scenario, based in part on soils that had been deliberately contaminated with lead in the lab, or where the lead had come from wastewater or sewage treatment. Lead recently-derived from petrol, car-batteries and lead-based paints is also known to have higher availability in soils, i.e. it's likely to end up in plants and the people who eat them. But the lead in allotment soils is different – it's aged and weathered, and has had plenty of time to end up in forms that are mostly unavailable to plants.

Other things that make lead safer in allotment soils are pH and organic matter. Lead, like most heavy metals, is much more soluble in acid soils, but the Newcastle allotments soils had an average pH of just above neutral. Lead also forms stable complexes with organic matter, again reducing its availability. In the Newcastle allotments, 'available' lead was strongly negatively correlated with organic matter content. We can expect most allotment soils, well limed and manured, to be similar.

In short, it's not really the amount of lead in soil that's important, but the form that lead takes, and lead in a typical allotment soil will mostly be locked up out of harm's way. Nevertheless, it pays to take sensible precautions to keep any lead *in the soil* out of your diet, for example by peeling and thoroughly washing all crops, and your hands, before eating.

More moon beliefs

A few years ago now, I suggested that sowing your seeds by the Kollerstrom/Maria Thun biodynamic moon calendar was unlikely to do you or your seeds much good. More than that, I pointed out that *Which? Gardening* have tested the moon-sowing idea fairly thoroughly (in fact twice), and failed to discover any difference between the moon-calendar's 'good' and 'bad' sowing dates.

I'm therefore happy to consider the subject closed. On the other hand, the feeling persists that something as big and obvious as the moon must be doing *something*. For example, my earlier article generated a fair amount of comment, including more than one mention of tides, plus an assertion by a barrister that custody officers and prison officers are aware of the effects of the full moon, and that a similar effect is well-known in lunatic asylums and mental hospitals.

Well, if everything that was 'well-known' was actually true, the world would be a very strange place indeed. But I'm always willing to learn, so I spent a while poking about among the published results of various lunar investigations. And by 'published', I mean 'published after peer review', thus eliminating the worst effects of wishful thinking and wilful self-delusion.

The results of my reading will take us a very long way from gardening, but let's start with something not too distant from horticulture. There is apparently a popular belief (I discovered a lot of popular beliefs) that the best time to forage for wild mushrooms is around the full moon.*

---

* One correspondent pointed out that this was when you were more likely to see them, but I'll leave you to work out the flaw in that argument.

To check this, Swiss mycologists looked at 1,715 precisely dated mycological records, collected between 1990 and 2007 in five long-term observation plots in Switzerland. The researchers found no relationship between lunar periodicity and mushroom yields, and concluded that the belief in such a relationship is a myth.

Another very widespread (indeed practically universal) belief is that lunar phases have some effect on the timing of childbirth. In fact the belief is so entrenched that it refuses to go away, and researchers keep coming back to it. In 2002, Austrian researchers published an analysis of all 2,760,362 children born in Austria between 1970 and 1999, i.e. 371 lunar cycles. In 2005, a team from Arizona published a study of all 167,956 births in Phoenix between 1995 and 2000. And in 2008 a German study looked at 6,725 deliveries from 1 January 2000 to 31 December 2006 at the Department of Obstetrics and Gynaecology of the University Medical School of Hannover. There are other modern studies too, but those three will do, since they all found the same: nothing.

The German study was, naturally, particularly thorough, and also showed no effect of moon phase on the need for an emergency caesarean section or on birthweight. Nor was there any effect of lunar position at the time of conception on baby gender (another popular belief, apparently). The German researchers also point out that assigning a birth to a specific phase of the moon can be tricky because the classic phases (new moon, waxing crescent moon, full moon and waning crescent moon) aren't the same length, and some early studies found more births at full moon because that phase was longer.

Nevertheless, one could always claim that in humans, one effect of modern life has been to eliminate a subtle effect of lunar cycles that existed before we took to spending all our time indoors gawping at Facebook. In the fairly sure knowledge that sheep are relatively unaffected by such influences, Spanish researchers analysed the timing of 68,127 lamb births in Spain over 37 consecutive lunar cycles, and as usual found nothing.

And in case you haven't had enough, other studies have looked for, but failed to find, any effect of the moon on epileptic seizures (in humans or in dogs and cats), psychiatric hospital admissions, emergency hospital admissions (in humans or pets), dog bites, heart attacks, surgical complications or violent crime.

To return to where I started, am I suggesting the moon does nothing at all? No, I'm not; in the sea, for example, where tidal rhythms are real and important, all kinds of things are synchronised with the moon. But on land, lunar effects appear to be a lot less important than many people think, so it's not too surprising that you can ignore them in the garden.

Do I think, by the way, that any of this will have any effect on those who believe in moon planting? No, not for a moment.

Mycorrhizas

Most plant species are mycorrhizal. That is, they form a symbiotic partnership with a soil fungus, which helps them to take up nutrients from the soil and also helps to protect them against drought and pathogens. The partnership is a very ancient one; the very earliest land plants appear to have been mycorrhizal.

Today, mycorrhizas come in two main sorts – and a few minor ones, which needn't concern us. Ectomycorrhizas form a sheath around the plant's roots and are found in conifers and many other large trees, such as beech, birch and oak. The fungus forms conspicuous reproductive structures (toadstools). Arbuscular mycorrhizal fungi (AMF for short) actually grow into the cells of the root and are found in a very wide range of plants, including most herbaceous plants and many trees and shrubs (e.g. apple, ash, cherry, dogwood and holly).

Because the mycorrhizal partnership is so obviously

beneficial to plants, plenty of people are keen to sell you mycorrhizas to add to the soil at planting time. But do they work? The British Standards Institution don't think so. In their new recommendations for planting young trees (BS 8545:2014), they say: 'Data from several independent trials demonstrate widely conflicting opinions as to their efficacy and therefore they should not be used as a matter of routine.' That 'matter of routine' suggests that there might be special circumstances in which they should be used, but since they don't offer any clues as to what those might be, I think we can take that as a straight 'no'. And since this British Standard is *the* guide to best practice for those who plant trees for a living, I think we should pay attention to what they say. Their support for things that *do* work is unambiguous; for example, on mulching: 'Mulches are beneficial to transplanting success and should be used wherever practical.'

Why are trials of mycorrhizas so inconsistent? An American study offers a clue. A team at Texas A&M University grew five different plants in containers in a sterile medium, some of them inoculated with mycorrhizas (they were all AMF plants), some of them not. Later they planted out the test plants into the ground and grew them on for two seasons. They checked if the plants' roots were actually infected with mycorrhizas, first at the end of the container stage, and then again at the end of the whole experiment.

The results were interesting. Inoculated plants became infected with AMF and, although the results were variable, generally grew a bit better than those without mycorrhizas at the planting-out stage. Thereafter, any advantage of the AMF-treated plants rapidly declined and had disappeared completely after two seasons in the ground. The reason was obvious when they checked for AMF infection: after two years, *all* the plants, inoculated or not, were equally infected with mycorrhizal fungi.

And therein, for the would-be mycorrhiza-user, lies the problem. Mycorrhizal fungi have wide host ranges (a single fungus species can infect lots of different plants) and their spores are pretty ubiquitous in soil; so ubiquitous that growing mycorrhiza-free plants for experimental purposes, other than in a sterile medium in a pot, is a challenge. For plants in ordinary garden soil, becoming infected with mycorrhizas is like catching a cold – whatever you do, you will in the end. This is only likely not to happen under fairly unusual conditions, where for some reason the natural mycorrhizal inoculum is missing or at least badly damaged. For example, establishing a garden on a former arable field, or trying to grow plants in pure builders' rubble (where absence of mycorrhizas may be the least of your problems). Bear in mind also that if you garden in a way that mycorrhizas don't like, for example too much digging, fungicides or fertiliser, adding more from a packet won't change that.

For plants that are going to spend a long time in a pot, in a sterile medium, it's possible that adding mycorrhizas may do some good. But don't count on it; when *Which? Gardening* last tested potting composts, the brand they tested that contains mycorrhizas turned out to be one of the worst performers. On the other hand, mycorrhizas are unlikely to do much harm, so if using them makes you feel better, go ahead.

Rockdust part 1

Many years ago now, I ventured the opinion that rockdust (ground volcanic rock) was unlikely to do very much for your garden. But that was, at the time, only my opinion, because I couldn't find any peer-reviewed research on the subject.

So I was pleased to find, in 2009, that Nicola Campbell had completed a PhD on rockdust at Glasgow University. And even more pleased that, in this electronic age, I didn't even have to go to Glasgow to read it. The rockdust we are talking about here, by the way, is promoted and sold by the Seer Centre, based near Pitlochry in Scotland. According to the Seer Centre, there's almost nothing rockdust can't do, including bigger yields, healthier crops, better flavour and improved resistance to pests, disease and drought.

Crucially, the field work for Nicola's PhD was carried out at the Seer Centre, with their full cooperation and assistance, and of course their rockdust. The thesis expresses profuse thanks to the Centre for their help with the project. This is important, because it means the Seer Centre was happy with the way the work was conducted and has no reason to complain about the results. Nicola's big field experiment also used rockdust at 40 tonnes per hectare (4kg per sq. m), at the top end of the recommended rate, so we can assume that if rockdust does anything, Nicola would have found it.

So what did she find? Well, you can read her thesis yourself, but there are 403 pages of it. Fortunately, a brief paragraph in the abstract tells you all you really need to know: 'No yield effects due to rockdust addition were apparent after 3 years of the field trial. In addition, rockdust did not impact on plant nutrient content nor did it affect the soil chemistry despite 3 years of weathering that was considered sufficient time to release nutrients to the soil.'

So rockdust does nothing at all, and again you don't have to look beyond the abstract to see why: 'Nutrient extractions showed that a high degree of rock weathering was required to release small quantities of trace elements from rockdust samples.' In short, it's tough to get anything out of rockdust, and even when you do it's mostly sodium, with small amounts of calcium and even smaller amounts of anything else. So the most rockdust might sometimes do is raise soil pH a little, although in Nicola's work it didn't.

I said before that the Seer Centre couldn't really complain about this trial. Nevertheless, when a complaint was made to the Advertising Standards Authority that the Centre's claims for rockdust didn't stand up, they rubbished the study, claiming the rockdust used was 'substandard'. Which rather begs the question of how you recognise a substandard rock, but in any case Nicola's thesis – a very careful, thorough piece of work – is clear: the rockdust she used is exactly the one that the Seer Centre sells in 20kg bags. The complaint to the ASA was upheld.

Maybe that would be enough for most people, but in 2013 a joint Scottish/Swedish team published the results of their work, carried out in Sweden but again using rockdust bought from Seer. Sometimes it can be a bit hard to tell what a scientific paper is trying to say, but the title of their paper is admirably direct: 'Addition of a volcanic rockdust to soils has no observable effects on plant yield and nutrient status or on soil microbial activity.' Which, if you read all of it, is exactly what their work shows: rockdust does nothing.

And that's that really. These were large-scale studies, carried out over three years, using rockdust at rates as high or higher than the maximum recommended, and both confirm my original hunch: soil is mostly rock already, so adding a bit more doesn't make much difference. But if you still feel like using it, at least it's unlikely to do any harm. Or as the Swedish study put it: 'As the rockdust had no nutrient or toxic effect it can probably be considered as an inert material which at least causes no harm but equally has no demonstrable ecological or agricultural benefit.'

Rockdust part 2

A while ago I reported the results of research showing that rockdust, widely sold as a soil additive and sometimes credited with almost magical properties, does exactly nothing. At least, it has no measurable effect on soil nutrients or plant yield. Nothing surprising about that; rockdust doesn't contain much that could be expected to affect plant growth, and the little it does contain is released only very slowly. It is, after all, rock, and if rocks broke down quickly the world (if it existed at all) would be a very different place.

But some of you may have noticed that rockdust has been in the news for other reasons; it might, just might, help us deal with climate change, or at least the major cause of climate change: too much CO_2. Apologies, but just a tiny bit of chemistry is required at this point. An awful lot of the world's volcanic rocks are silicates of calcium or magnesium, and as these weather, they react with CO_2 to release bicarbonate and calcium or magnesium ions. The bicarbonate (now containing the CO_2) mostly ends up in the sea, which is a much better place for it than the atmosphere. Bicarbonate even helps to reduce ocean acidification, so everyone is happy.

This process happens all the time, without any help from us, and in fact it soaks up about 2.5% of annual fossil fuel CO_2 emissions to the atmosphere. Which is where rockdust comes in; if we added a lot more finely-divided (and therefore more reactive) rock to the world's soils, could we use up a lot more CO_2?

The only place this has been tried on a large scale is the Hubbard Brook Experimental Forest in New Hampshire. Hubbard Brook is essentially a giant outdoor laboratory that has been used since 1955 to study everything from forest management to acid rain; the work there has resulted in over 2,000 scientific papers. In short it's the perfect place to study the large-scale effects of silicate rocks on the carbon cycle and, fortunately, someone has.

In 1999, 3.5 tons/ha of the calcium silicate mineral, wollastonite, was added to one of several catchment areas at Hubbard Brook and the impact monitored for the next twelve years.

The effect on carbon sequestration wasn't the main objective of the experiment, but along the way the wollastonite did approximately double the amount of CO_2 leaving the catchment as bicarbonate. So if you could add ground silicate rock to *all* the world's soils, you could expect to soak up about another 2.5% of global fossil fuel emissions.

Which is easy to say, but not at all easy to do. In the first place, rock is heavy stuff, and most of the world's soils are relatively inaccessible, so you could only add crushed rock to soils where the infrastructure for delivering bulky material like fertiliser already exists – in practice, agricultural soils in developed countries. And although there's no theoretical limit to the supply, we are talking about an awful lot of rock; quite a few large mountains would have to be levelled to supply the rock needed, not forgetting the CO_2 emitted during the mining, crushing and transport. Finally, the cost would be about $10,000 per ton of carbon absorbed, which is very expensive compared to other proposed carbon-sequestration technologies.

Nor is rockdust perfect for the job; unlike wollastonite, which is more or less pure calcium silicate, the rockdust widely sold in the UK contains less calcium (or magnesium), so doesn't work as well. To sum up, not only will rockdust not help you to grow better veg or roses, a couple of bags on your garden won't help to save the planet either. If you want to garden your way to a smaller carbon footprint, you already know what to do: go easy on the digging, grow some of your own food, plant a tree and make (and use) as much compost as you can.

INTERESTING THINGS ABOUT PLANTS

A surprise by the back door

There is little doubt that Britain's native flora is in decline. Figures from the charity Plantlife International show that the average British county loses a species of wild plant every two or three years. There's also not much doubt about the identity of the main losers: typical examples include burnt orchid, field gentian, sheep's-bit, butterwort, wild thyme, sundew and petty whin. In other words, short, slow-growing plants of relatively undisturbed (but often grazed), nutrient-poor habitats.

The reasons are clear too. Sometimes straightforward habitat destruction, by the construction of houses or roads. But more often drastic habitat modification, such as the draining of wetlands, or the 'improvement' of old pastures or meadows by the use of fertilisers and herbicides. One insidious threat to plants of nutrient-poor habitats is the steady rain of fixed nitrogen ('acid rain') from power generation and vehicles.

How likely are gardens to provide a refuge for such plants? Not very, is the short answer. Gardens are generally too disturbed and – especially – far too fertile. Much has been written, for example, about how difficult it is to create a traditional wildflower meadow on a typical fertile garden soil. That's not to say that rare native plants aren't found in gardens; they are, but only because we cultivate them.

For instance, in her 30-year study of her Leicester garden, Jennifer Owen grew (among others) Jacob's ladder, shrubby cinquefoil, henbane, box and clustered bellflower – all rare natives. There are plenty of other rare, attractive natives that we could grow in our gardens, but whether such cultivation makes any real contribution to their conservation is a moot point.

Native plants do turn up in gardens of their own accord, but it's interesting to look at a few of the long list of species that did so in Owen's garden: creeping buttercup, nettle, fat hen, broad-leaved dock, garlic mustard, hogweed, bindweed, goosegrass, sow thistle, dandelion and ragwort. You get the picture; not the sort of plants that are in any obvious need of help, from gardeners or anyone else. In the whole 30 years, no native plant that could remotely be described as rare or declining turned up spontaneously in Owen's garden. This is hardly surprising; such plants tend to be confined to fragments of 'unimproved' landscape that are remote from towns and cities, and many are notoriously poorly-dispersed. On the very rare occasion that their seeds do make it into a garden, they usually find conditions are not to their liking. The 61 Sheffield gardens we looked at for the BUGS project tell the same story: rare natives turned up occasionally (e.g. baneberry, mountain everlasting, spurge laurel, roseroot), but they always gave every sign of being planted.

It's thus axiomatic that rare native plants hardly ever turn up spontaneously in gardens. Of course, there are always going to be exceptions, but I was still surprised last year to find one – specifically, a twayblade – right outside my back door. Twayblade (*Neottia* – formerly *Listera* – *ovata*) is admittedly one of our commoner orchids, but no orchid is exactly common. In fact the BSBI database has no records at all for the city of Sheffield, although there is the odd record just outside the built-up area. The only place nearby where twayblade is at all frequent is in the limestone dales of the Peak District National Park, a good half-hour's drive away.

My plant is under a large *Viburnum* × *bodnantense*, with nothing much for company in summer, although there's a patch of wood anemone in spring. The spot is also undisturbed, with a nice deep layer of leaf mould, and has never had any fertiliser. My soil is a bit acid, but I can imagine the twayblade's preference for limestone might be satisfied by run-off from the house's concrete apron. It must have been there for a while; twayblades are slow-growing and like all orchids have tiny seeds, so seedlings take at least seven years to reach flowering size.

The minute seeds of orchids are widely dispersed, so I can only conclude that one blew in, or perhaps came in on a walking boot. Either way, it found a nice, undisturbed spot with no competition, and presumably the cooperative fungal partner that all orchids need. Which tells me – well, what does it tell me? That you never know what might be lurking in undisturbed corners of gardens, and that there's no limit to the surprises the natural world can spring on us. And more generally, that rules were made to be broken, and that it always pays to keep your eyes open.

Darwin on twining

Even before they do any climbing, twining stems revolve and, once they hit a support, this revolving leads naturally to twining in whichever direction they had previously been revolving. But which direction is that? Darwin carefully observed numerous twiners, classifying them as twining 'with the sun' or 'against the sun'. There's nothing wrong with those labels, but they do mean different things in the northern and southern hemispheres, so it's probably a better idea to have a description of twining direction that works anywhere. A commonly-used terminology is clockwise or anticlockwise, but that's even worse. Because now, instead of just knowing which hemisphere you're in, you need to know whether you're on the floor looking *up* a climbing stem, or up a ladder looking *down*. Does the earth rotate clockwise or anticlockwise? It depends which pole you're looking at. A better way to describe twining direction is as *left-handed* or *right-handed*. In other words, does the twining stem cross the support from lower left to upper right (right-handed), or from lower right to upper left (left-handed). This always gives the same result, irrespective of where you're standing, or which hemisphere you're in.

There are two popular notions about which way plants twine. One, probably the more widespread, is that plants track the apparent daily east-west movement of the sun across the sky. Indeed only the other day, I read a newspaper description of a hop grower carefully helping the young hop stems to twine so that they track the sun (as if they needed any help, or that you could possibly persuade them to do anything else). The other idea is that it's all determined by the Coriolis effect, which is what makes your bathwater drain in different directions (allegedly) in the northern and southern hemispheres. The latter hypothesis predicts right-handed twining in the northern hemisphere and left-handed twining in the southern hemisphere. Predictions of the sun hypothesis are more complicated, but you would still expect the direction of twining to vary with hemisphere and latitude.

In 2007 New Zealand ecologist Angela Moles published a paper showing that about 92% of the world's twining plants twine in a right-handed helix, and this is true everywhere on the planet, so both hypotheses are wrong, and hops are in the small left-handed minority. But Darwin's observations, 140 years earlier, already strongly hinted at a preponderance of right-handed climbers; of the 40 species he studied, 27 were right-handed and thirteen left-handed (if the appropriate statistical test had been invented at the time, this difference would have proved to be significant: i.e. the proportions of left- and right-handed twiners was not random). In fact Darwin seems to suggest that this was old news even then: 'A greater number of twiners revolve in a course opposed to that of the sun, or to the hands of a watch, than in the reversed course, and, consequently, the majority, *as is well known*, ascend their supports from left to right' (my italics).

Curiously, Darwin noted: 'I have seen no instance of two species of the same genus twining in opposite directions, and such cases must be rare.' One of the species he describes is *Wisteria sinensis*, which he correctly notes is right-handed. The Chinese wisteria was introduced to Britain in 1816, and by 1835 was widely available, so it's not surprising that Darwin knew it. Down House, Darwin's home in Kent, is today home to a large Chinese wisteria, and the romantic in me would like to believe that it was planted by Darwin himself. Unfortunately, although old watercolours and black-and-white photographs show Down House covered by climbers, these are all long gone, and we don't know what they were. A photograph from as recently as 1994 shows Down House completely devoid of climbers, so its present covering must all date from its acquisition in 1996 by English Heritage, and it may just be an accident that the wisteria is the 'right' one.*

It's a pity that Darwin was writing just too soon to be aware of the Japanese wisteria, *W. floribunda*, which wasn't introduced from Japan (via the Netherlands) until the 1870s, so he was unaware of its left-handed twining (which thus allows it to be separated from its Chinese cousin, even when completely leafless).

Undoubtedly, however, Darwin was right that two species in the same genus twining in opposite directions must be rare; I don't know of any apart from wisteria. Collectors of botanical trivia will be delighted to learn that any hybrid of Japanese wisteria inherits its twining direction from that parent.

---

* No, English Heritage inform me, they were careful to choose the wisteria Darwin would have grown. This article is an extract from *Darwin's Most Wonderful Plants: Darwin's Botany Today*, published on 1 November 2018 by Profile Books.

How to date a meadow

As every schoolboy (and girl) knows (or as every schoolboy *should* know, in an ideal world), you can date a hedge very roughly by counting the number of different kinds of trees and shrubs in it. Older hedges – on average – have more species in them.

But just suppose you wanted to know the age of a *meadow*. Counting the number of different plants in a meadow is a job for an expert, and it wouldn't help anyway, since there's no simple relationship between number of species and age.

So how do you find the age of a meadow? I confess I wouldn't have had a clue until quite recently. But the other day, while looking for something else altogether, I came across a bit of overlooked research from a few years ago in the journal *Annals of Botany* that tells you the answer. Actually it may not have been overlooked at all, but it was certainly overlooked by me. And I think – I really think – you should know about it. It uses some really neat biology, it's dead simple, and better still, it works.

The principle is that as any organism grows, and its cells divide, they accumulate tiny genetic mistakes: mutations. If these mutations accumulate at a constant rate we have the basis, in principle at least, of a clock. But we need the right plant, and the right mutation.

111

Buttercups are a good choice. But not just any old buttercup, because sexual reproduction, followed by establishment of a new plant from a seed, resets the mutational clock to zero. So a plant that regularly reproduces by seed is no use; most of its individuals will be younger than the meadow, often much younger. We have three common species of buttercup, and two of them, the bulbous buttercup and the meadow buttercup, reproduce frequently by seed. But the creeping buttercup does not, it mostly reproduces vegetatively (hence the name). So you can be reasonably certain that the creeping buttercups in a meadow are about the same age as the meadow. With a decent wildflower book and a bit of practice, the three buttercups are easy to tell apart. Creeping buttercup is the annoying weed that grows in your lawn, and your borders too, given half a chance.

The right mutation has to do something that we can measure easily. Most mutations either don't do much, or what they do isn't easily measured. It turns out that the perfect mutation is one that increases the number of petals in the flower.

So, now we have the right plant, plus the right mutation, finding the age of a meadow could hardly be simpler. Look at 100 randomly-chosen creeping buttercup flowers and count how many have more than the regulation five petals. Every flower with extra petals equals roughly seven years. So if you looked at 100 flowers and fourteen of them had extra petals, your meadow is about 100 years old. Technically of course, we've found the age of the creeping buttercups in the meadow, but we're assuming that's the same thing.*

Good, eh? Just the thing to keep the kids out of trouble on a country walk while you're eating your picnic, plus they learn some science and some history, and you get to show how clever you are.

Leaning trees

A tree adds a certain something to a garden, and it's always a good idea to try to fit one in, even if your garden is only modest. Owners of large gardens, of course, can accommodate bigger trees. But whether your tree is large or small,

---

* I should also have pointed out that in the past, meadows were sometimes ploughed and reseeded, in which case it's the time since then that you're measuring. The 'buttercup method' can only give you the meadow's ultimate age if it has never suffered any major disturbance. Also, when the method was being tested, there were very few meadows that could be reliably dated to more than 200 years, so it has only been validated for meadows up to 200 years old.

unless it's had some kind of accident, or your garden is very windy, it's a good bet that it's more or less vertical.

Which may seem like stating the blindingly obvious, except that plants generally grow towards the light, and unless you live within 23.5° of the equator, sunlight never comes from directly overhead. So maybe trees – in the northern hemisphere – should lean a bit south? But natural selection has taught trees that the advantages of leaning towards the prevailing light (more even illumination of the crown) are far outweighed by the disadvantages (high probability of falling over).

In short, plants respond to both light and gravity, usually growing towards the light and away from the centre of the earth. But for tall plants, gravity always has the upper hand. In fact, trees have clever mechanisms for detecting (and correcting) the uneven forces generated in the trunk by any tendency to lean.

But one of the wonderful things about the natural world is that natural selection doesn't always come up with the same answer to the same question, and odd ways of doing things sometimes persist here and there. So no real surprise that there *is* a leaning tree: *Araucaria columnaris*, or Cook pine (and no, before you check, it's not April fool's day). Cook pine is endemic to New Caledonia but is widely grown in warm climates throughout the world. A recent paper in the journal *Ecology* describes how Cook pines lean towards the equator, at an angle that increases as you get further north or south. A picture in the paper of leaning Cook pines in California makes you realise what a strange place the world would be if this habit were widespread.

How has Cook pine managed to get away with this peculiar behaviour? Well, New Caledonia has a remarkable diversity of conifers, including thirteen endemic species of *Araucaria*, so maybe it had more chances than most of coming up with something unusual. Certainly New Caledonia seems to have a habit of trying coniferous experiments that never caught on anywhere else in the world, for example it is home to the world's only parasitic conifer. Also, since it's only about 22° S, native trees don't lean all that much – it's only when you get to somewhere like California (around 35° N) that the lean becomes really noticeable.

What are your chances of growing a Cook pine? Not good I'm afraid; like its close relative Norfolk Island pine (*A. heterophylla*), it's really too tender to grow outdoors in Britain. The only decent specimen used to be on Tresco, but it was killed by a bad winter in 1987. In any case, even if you could, it would probably just fall over.

Two authors chasing a ghost

Most of us – I hope – would agree that plants are just the most wonderful things. And that although it's hard to beat looking at beautiful plants, or even better growing them, reading about plants and the people who love them is pretty good too. Which is why the last year has been such a treat, with not one but two books from two of our most celebrated plant lovers: Peter Marren and Roy Lancaster.

Roy Lancaster's *My Life With Plants* does exactly what it says on the tin – a canter through a life spent growing, admiring, searching for, and writing and talking about plants. In short, a life well spent, and you get the impression Roy wouldn't want to change a minute of it. Peter Marren's book, in contrast, is about a single year in his life, searching for the last 50 British wild plants that had previously eluded him. Its title, *Chasing the Ghost*, refers to the ghost orchid, *Epipogium aphyllum*, by common consent Britain's most elusive wildflower.

The two books, on the face of it, don't sound all that similar, and yet they both begin in much the same way, with a book. In Roy's case with the *Flora of Bolton* (his home town), in Peter's case with the Rev. Keble Martin's *Concise British Flora*, the first book to bring colour pictures of wildflowers to the general public. Both authors loved ticking things off a list, and in Roy's book there's a wonderful picture of a page of the Bolton *Flora* with his annotations. As gardeners, we associate Roy's name with garden plants and exotic locations like the Himalayas, but like many plant lovers his passion began at home. I defy you to read his description of an early trip to Silverdale ('a name ... akin to that of the Elven Kingdom of Lothlórien in Tolkien's *Lord of the Rings*') without wanting to catch a train there right now.

In Peter Marren's case, it was the realisation that he had ticked off all but 50 of our (possibly) native plants in his battered copy of the *Concise British Flora* that gave him the idea for 'The Quest': find all the missing fifty, in a single year. The story (maybe a better description would be the odyssey) is riveting, with appalling weather and near-death experiences, but also sublime moments and many meetings with friends (plant and human) old and new. Many of the plants he sought are inconspicuous to the point of invisibility, which is one reason they had previously escaped him. For example, the tiny strapwort: 'Our small colony contained perhaps a quarter of all the strapworts in Britain. You could fit the entire population on a kitchen table and still have room for the plates.' But time and again Peter is surprised by the beauty he finds: 'Strapwort, to my surprise, is quite nice ... crimson bracts [and] little green stars.' He was even 'entranced' by pedunculate sea-purslane, which takes some doing.

Another surprising convergence between the two books is the ghost orchid, a plant of almost mythical unpredictability, and so rare that it has been officially declared extinct in Britain – at almost the same moment that it unexpectedly turned up again. In short a plant that any keen botanist or gardener would give quite a lot to see. Did either of our heroes ever succeed in seeing one? To find out, get both books on your Christmas list now, or get them even quicker if you have a birthday coming up.

Orange is the new blacklisted

If gardeners think about genetically-modified garden plants at all, they perhaps think it would be nice (although, frankly, also a bit weird) to have a genuinely blue rose, or (weirder still) a red daffodil. The funny thing is, we've been there, or somewhere very like it, and not recently either.

In a paper in the journal *Nature* in 1987, a team at the Max Planck Institute for Plant Breeding Research in Cologne showed that inserting a maize gene into a petunia enabled it to make the pigment pelargonidin. Pelargonidin, as its name suggests, helps to make pelargoniums (and strawberries and raspberries) red. In a petunia, its effect is a kind of salmon colour. Dutch agribusiness giant Syngenta licensed the technology and by 1995 had developed a vivid orange petunia – a colour that no petunia has ever managed if left to itself. The new petunia was trialled in Florida but Syngenta never sought market approval; in any case, they couldn't have been sold in Europe, where there has long been a *de facto* ban on growing GM plants of any kind. One of many things that we could change after Brexit – if we choose to.

So that was that – or was it? Fast forward to 2015, when Finnish plant biologist Teemu Teeri noticed some orange petunias in a planter outside Helsinki railway station. He took a piece back to the lab and eventually confirmed that the petunias had foreign genes matching those described in the 1987 paper. Teeri mentioned his discovery to a former student who now works for the Finnish Board for Gene Technology and soon the Finnish food safety regulator, Evira, was calling for eight orange petunia varieties to be removed from sale. The EU Commission quickly asked other EU members to follow suit.

How did the orange petunias escape from the lab into the marketplace? No one knows, or at least no one is admitting they know. But it's not too surprising; companies merge, personnel move on, and before you know it no one knows where seeds came from. In all probability no one is to blame and it was simply an honest mistake. But it's clear that although several varieties have been available for the best part of a decade, there is no authorisation for their sale and suppliers must destroy them. Thompson & Morgan have already stated: 'We're not selling any. We've withdrawn them from sale.'

Orange petunias are not the advance guard of a wave of GM flowers – this looks like a one-off mistake. Nor, given the low probability of gaining approval to sell them, are companies likely to want to invest in the research needed to produce GM garden plants. Getting their fingers burned with orange petunias, albeit unwittingly, won't encourage them either.

But as everyone is at pains to point out, orange petunias are about as harmless as it gets; as the Horticultural Trades Association puts it: 'orange-coloured petunias pose no threat to people, animals or the environment.' So what should you do if you have a hanging basket full of petunia 'African Sunset'? While I'm sure that not immediately incinerating them must be infringing some regulation or other, I think a knock on the door from the horticultural police is extremely unlikely. Just don't make the mistake of exhibiting them at your local flower show.

And look on the bright side – now that there's a warrant out for their arrest, continuing to grow petunia 'Orange Punch' brings with it a frisson of danger that you don't normally associate with growing petunias.

A winter plant hunt

Every year the BSBI (Botanical Society of Britain and Ireland) organises a New Year Plant Hunt (NYPH). Its mission is simple: identify and count all the plants you can find in flower during a three-hour walk in a four-day period over New Year. The results for 2018 have now been collated and analysed, and can be seen on an interactive map on the BSBI website.

The plant most frequently found (streets ahead of its nearest rival, and surely a great pub quiz question) was common daisy, *Bellis perennis*. But as ever, much of the fun is in the detail, which quickly reveals that location is crucial. I write from south Devon, and one of the longest lists comes from just down the road from here on the coast at Brixham. On the other hand, a list from Two Bridges in the middle of Dartmoor, only a few miles away but a long way uphill, consists of a single plant: common gorse. I'm not surprised; however hard you look, I suspect it wouldn't have been easy to get into double figures at Two Bridges.

Nationally, the longest and third longest lists come from sites a few miles apart in the far west of Cornwall, while second place goes to a list from Swanage. Mind you, the winners, from Phillack on the north coast of Cornwall, got up to 114 species by not only displaying an ability to distinguish *Conyza floribunda* (Bilbao fleabane) from *C. canadensis* (Canadian fleabane), but also recognised plants the rest of us have never heard of, such as *Polypogon viridis* (water bent) and *Cyperus eragrostis* (pale galingale).

But what the results mostly illustrate is that if you count or measure *anything* for long enough, interesting patterns emerge. The NYPH is only in its seventh year, but it's already clear, climate change notwithstanding, that what really matters is the weather in the period leading up to the hunt. The number of people taking part has risen dramatically, but compared to the previous three years, the average number of plants each group found was much lower in 2017 and 2018. Inspection of the weather records reveals that those three hunts were preceded by an unusually mild autumn/early winter, while the weather during the last two years has been much more normal, i.e. cold.

The total number of species found in flower this year was a whopping 532, which is far more than reference books would lead us to expect. It's tempting to assume that this is a much larger number than would have been found in the past, but since no one was counting in, say, 1950 or 1960, the long-term pattern will only emerge when we've been doing this for quite a few more years.

What is already clear, however, is that the bulk of the 'extra' plants are not early, but late. That is, only a few of the unexpected plants found in flower at New Year are ones that we would normally expect to find in flower later in the spring. Mostly the extra plants are summer- or autumn-flowering species 'left over' from the previous year. In fact spring-flowering plants generally need a period of cold before they can flower, and if winters become significantly warmer, it may even be that we will find *fewer* spring plants in flower at New Year in future.

One thing's for sure, the NYPH is now an important fixture in the botanical calendar, and everyone is welcome to take part – you don't have to be a BSBI member or an experienced botanist, and even nil records are important, so it's OK if you don't find anything. Plenty of tips to get you started on the BSBI website, so make a note in your diary for 2019.

Slippery plants

Smooth surfaces, self-evidently, are easier to keep clean than rough ones. The paint on a shiny new car is easier to keep clean than that on an old banger. A smooth, polished table can be cleaned more easily than a rough, rustic wooden table. I'm even tempted to suggest that less mud seems to stick to politicians of a smooth, shiny aspect.

Plants, you will not be surprised to hear, are completely different. Water runs off some plants like a duck's back, and such plants tend to have leaves with rough surfaces. It's not the sort of roughness that you can easily see, because it's on a very small scale, but it's there nevertheless. Water-repellent leaves tend to be covered with minute lumps and bumps (technically, papillae) that are anything from 5–100 μm tall, or about the width of a human hair (1 μm is one millionth of a metre).

To understand how these papillae work, you need to understand how water works. Water has a powerful surface tension, which means it behaves as though it has an elastic skin. Because of this, water very much wants to form spherical drops, and to make it do anything else is quite hard work. So wetting a surface, which involves persuading water drops to abandon their desire to be spherical and to spread out instead, requires the input of energy. This energy is supplied by the bonding between the molecules of the water drop and those of the surface it's sitting on (technically, adsorption). Which is where the papillae come in, because they prevent the water drop from contacting anything other than the tips of the papillae. In other words, there's hardly any contact between the water and the leaf, and thus very little energy to be gained by adsorption, so the water stays in a drop, and the leaf stays dry.

Such water drops easily roll off the edges of leaves and fall to the ground, and as they do so, something remarkable happens – something that shows just how clever plants really are. Water-repellency is greatly aided by a coating of wax, because wax is extremely hydrophobic, or 'water-hating' (but the wax is not enough on its own – the papillae are essential). Crucially, all the muck that accumulate on leaves (soil, dust, pollution, fungal spores) consists of particles that are more easily wetted than wax. They're also, like everything else, balanced on the tips of the papillae, so they're not strongly attached to the leaf. As a water drop rolls over them, it tends to pick them up and carry them away, leaving the leaf not only dry, but clean. Scientists have tried coating leaves with all manner of contaminants, from dried soil and dust to photocopier toner and mould and fern spores. In every case the result is the same – after a light shower, rough, water-repellent leaves are completely clean, while smooth leaves stay dirty.

And for leaves, cleanliness is crucial. Dirt particles can gum up the stomata through which leaves absorb CO_2, and in bright sunlight heavy contamination can absorb excess heat, leading to the leaf overheating. Most disease spores also need water to germinate, so find it hard to infect plants with dry leaves.

Leaves vary widely in water repellency, but the king of self-cleaning leaves is the sacred lotus, *Nelumbo nucifera*, which is practically botanical Teflon and has long been a symbol of purity in eastern philosophy and religion. As the

Hindu *Bhagavad Gita* says: 'One who performs his duty without attachment, surrendering the results unto the Supreme Lord, is unaffected by sinful action, as the lotus is untouched by water.'

To end on a practical note, the wax coating of water-repellent leaves is relatively fragile and is easily damaged by abrasion or by some chemicals. The surfactants found in water-based pesticides are there to improve the uptake of an active ingredient through the cuticle, but they also damage the wax layer. This damage increases the wettability of the leaf and may increase the likelihood of infection by fungal pathogens. One more reason, if you needed one, to think twice about using pesticides.

A floral conundrum

Flowers have a problem. They really want to attract lots of the right kind of insects to distribute their pollen. At the same time, they don't want to attract the wrong kind of insects – the sort that might eat their flowers rather than pollinate them. But if plants produce scents to attract pollinators, herbivores are just as likely to detect them and follow the trail to its source.

The problem is acute because flowers are quite likely to be both tasty and nutritious (less tough than leaves, for example), while losing them to herbivores is disastrous: no flowers, no seeds. How flowers – specifically, petunias – get round this problem has been investigated by a team of American and German researchers; their findings are reported in the journal *Ecology Letters*.

They used a white-flowered petunia, known to be pollinated by nocturnal hawkmoths (although red- or purple-flowered ones aren't). The main flower-eaters at their experimental site in Utah are a beetle and a cricket, both of which also feed at night, which prevents the plant from using the old trick of releasing a scent when pollinators are most active (often during the day), and not when most herbivores are about (often at night). Like most hawkmoth-pollinated plants, the petunia is stuck with being scented at night.

Maybe, they reasoned, the petunia releases not only scents that attract hawkmoths, but others that repel herbivores. The chemical that petunias use to attracts hawkmoths is known to be methyl benzoate, which has a pleasant, fruity smell. It also attracts humans (it's used in perfumery), and the two flower-eating insects as well. Until recently the idea that flowers also produce herbivore-repellent scents would have been difficult to investigate, but modern molecular methods make it relatively straightforward. The biochemical pathways that produce petunia floral scents are well understood, and genetically-modified lines exist that have had different branches of the pathway 'silenced', making them unable to produce particular scent chemicals.

When the researchers grew five of these lines, it was immediately obvious that two of them suffered much higher levels of floral herbivory than the others. These two produced normal amounts of methyl benzoate, but failed to produce two other chemicals produced by normal plants: isoeugenol and benzyl benzoate, implicating both as herbivore repellents. To make sure, the researchers carried out further experiments in which they artificially replaced both chemicals, and showed that this reduced floral herbivory back to normal levels.

How do these repellents work? They could just prevent the herbivores from visiting flowers at all, but observations of flowers shows this is not the case – normal flowers, able to produce both repellents, were visited by just as many beetles and crickets as the flowers that couldn't produce either. Thus they seem to act over only a short distance, i.e. herbivores have no trouble finding flowers, presumably by following the methyl benzoate trail as usual, but the two repellents seem to make them less likely to tuck in once they've arrived. Weirdly, although isoeugenol and benzyl benzoate clearly put insects off their food, both are attractive to humans; The Body Shop and Lush (and many others) put both in shampoo and other products.

Interestingly, producing repellent scents doesn't exhaust the ways petunias have found to try to avoid attracting insects that might eat their flowers. Red-flowered petunias have given up producing floral scents altogether and are instead pollinated by hummingbirds, which aren't interested in how flowers smell, or even if they smell at all.

Ripe fruit

When is a fruit ripe? A peach, say. Well, we know when we taste it, but by then it's too late if we realise it should have been left to ripen for a bit longer. During ripening, there are internal changes, mainly involving more sugar; a ripe peach is sweeter than an unripe one. But in terms of things you can detect from the outside, there are two main changes: in firmness, and colour. Firmness is what we're trying to estimate when we pick up a peach and gently squeeze it. But although it's fairly easy to detect a really unripe, hard peach, degrees of softness are hard to distinguish without damaging the fruit. Commercial penetrometers have the same problem; they are very good at measuring ripeness, but only at the cost of punching a hole in the fruit. And firmness really is crucial, since really hard peaches will never ripen properly, while there's only a short period in which peaches that *will* ripen can be stored and handled without bruising.

Colour is a better bet, since it can be measured without damaging the fruit. With modern technology, this can be done very accurately, but to automatically (and quickly) measure the ripeness of large numbers of fruit, something relatively cheap and cheerful is required. The prime candidate is reflection of red light, which essentially measures degradation of chlorophyll, a reliable indicator of ripening. Chlorophyll absorbs red light, so as chlorophyll is lost, less red is absorbed and more is reflected. Even better than red alone is the red/infra-red ratio, which corrects for variation in lighting, since reflection of infra-red doesn't change much during ripening.

But there are harder problems than measuring ripeness. We all know a ripe tomato when we see one, but there's always that moment, towards the end of the season, when you start to wonder if the green fruit left on the plant will ever turn red. Green fruit can be ripened off the plant, all they need is warmth and maybe a bit of ethylene (easily provided by a ripe banana), although tomatoes ripened 'on the vine' are generally reckoned to have a better flavour. But the change in colour from green to red is only the final stage of tomato ripening. In fact, tomatoes become 'physiologically ripe' while still green, and 'ripe' green tomatoes will turn red, while 'unripe' green tomatoes will not. But even to the most skilled observer, all green tomatoes look the same. Picking green tomatoes that won't turn red is disappointing, and for commercial growers it's an expensive mistake.

Although ripe and unripe green tomatoes look the same, analysis of the light reflected from them shows that ripe and unripe green tomatoes really do look different, it's just that the difference is invisible to the human eye. As in peaches, the change of colour is partly breakdown of chlorophyll, but also formation of two carotenoids: β-carotene (yellow) and lycopene (red), and it looks like it's possible to pick up the earliest stages of this change. At the moment this is too expensive for commercial use, but in the future it might save a lot of wasted tomatoes.

But peaches and tomatoes are easy compared to some fruits. We know what happens as avocados ripen (oil content goes up, firmness and water content go down), but none of this is very obvious from outside. Spectral methods have been tried for avocados, but don't work as well as for fruits with more obvious colour changes. Flotation (avocados become less dense as they ripen) and even nuclear magnetic resonance have also been tried, but perhaps the most promising recent candidate is ultrasound; the flesh of a ripe avocado attenuates an ultrasonic signal more than an unripe one. Speaking as a victim of too many dodgy 'ready to eat' avocados, a handy device that will tell me (or someone, anyway) how ripe they really are can't come soon enough.

Pact with devil's ivy clears the air

Chlorinated hydrocarbons are widely used as solvents and as raw materials for the synthesis of all kinds of useful products, such as cleaning agents and pesticides. Huge quantities of vinyl chloride are manufactured every year, nearly all of it to make PVC. Naturally these chemicals escape into the environment, ending up in ground water and eventually in drinking water, and since many are both toxic and persistent, there's a lot of interest in finding ways of getting rid of them.

As long ago as 2000, American researchers had the idea of introducing the mammalian enzyme cytochrome P450 2E1 into plants; this enzyme, found in large amounts in the liver, is really good at oxidizing a whole bunch of nasty chemicals, including trichloroethylene, ethylene dibromide, carbon tetrachloride, chloroform and vinyl chloride. These experiments, using GM tobacco with the added liver gene, were spectacularly successful. More recently, field trials using GM poplars with the same gene have also shown promise.

All this made researchers interested in other kinds of pollution think about the potential of GM plants. The air in our homes is full of all sorts of volatile organic compounds (VOCs) from detergents, cleaning products, air fresheners, paints, furniture and carpets. Using low-VOC products (especially sprays) and effective ventilation can help, but it's hard to avoid these chemicals entirely, and all the evidence shows they're not good for us.

So, maybe plants can come to our rescue? To find out, researchers in Seattle tried putting P450 2E1 into the houseplant *Epipremnum aureum* – Ceylon creeper or devil's ivy; their findings were published recently in *Environmental Science & Technology*. Since the same researchers had already shown that GM tobacco dealt really well with some common airborne pollutants, they weren't surprised to discover that their GM houseplant did too; tested on benzene and chloroform, it removed most of the former and all of the latter from the air in just a few days.

P450 2E1 isn't the complete answer to air pollution. For example it's no use against formaldehyde, which is either present in, or produced by, almost everything from paint to plywood and from cooking to computers. But there's a gene for that too: the *faldh* gene from the bacterium *Brevibacillus brevis* has been shown to work well against formaldehyde in GM tobacco plants. Nor do you need more than one plant; both genes – and others if necessary – could easily be inserted into the same plant, to produce an all-purpose pollution-remover. It's also worth remembering that these genes don't just remove these pollutants from the air, they actually destroy them completely, leaving only water, CO_2 and a few chloride ions.

Is there anything special about *Epipremnum*? No – the researchers chose it for the entirely pragmatic reasons that a published protocol for genetically modifying it already existed, and that it hardly ever flowers in cultivation, so the chance of the modified gene escaping was more or less zero. *Epipremnum* is in the arum family, like many other houseplant favourites including *Philodendron* and *Monstera* (Swiss cheese plant), so there's no reason why we couldn't develop a whole fleet of pollution-destroying houseplants. Except that GM plants are still effectively banned in the EU; overturning that ban might (but only might) be one of the few unambiguously positive results of Brexit.

Gooseberries; aliens in our midst

A book I really enjoyed reading last year was one of the latest in Collins' *New Naturalist* series: *Alien Plants* by Clive Stace and Mick Crawley. Every chapter told me something

I didn't know, but perhaps my favourite was 'Our top fifty-two neophytes'. Neophytes are what botanists call alien plants that only escaped into the wild after 1500 (introductions that escaped into the wild before that date are called archaeophytes).

First of all, why 52? Well, almost the only really objective measure of commonness is to count how many *hectads* a plant is found in. A hectad is a 10 × 10 km Ordnance Survey grid square, and there are about 3,859 hectads in the British Isles. So a reasonable definition of a common neophyte is one found in at least one-third of them (1,286), of which there are 52, or just 2.87% of the total. The great majority of neophytes are much less common; in fact only just over a third are found in more than 1% of hectads.

Most neophytes started out as garden plants, and many would be a lot commoner if you included planted specimens in gardens, but we're talking here about abundance in the wild. Nevertheless, the authors of *Alien Plants* are sorry to have to report that top of the list is not an escaped garden plant, but the very unprepossessing pineapple weed (*Matricaria discoidea*). First reported in 1869, pineapple weed is now a universal inhabitant of trampled bare ground; indeed it's the only neophyte that's found in over 90% of hectads.

Number 2 on the list, just short of 90%, is sycamore, and number 3 is snowberry, *Symphoricarpos albus*. Already you can see that our commonest neophytes have very little in common, and are a complete mixture of weeds, herbaceous perennials, shrubs and trees. You may have been slightly surprised to find snowberry so near the top, but neither the second commonest alien shrub (*Rhododendron ponticum*) nor the fourth (buddleja) will surprise you much. But the third might: *Ribes uva-crispa*, gooseberry.

Gooseberry is so common in hedgerows and scrub that you might have assumed, if you ever thought about it at all, that it was native. In fact gooseberry has often been claimed as a native; Richard Mabey, in *Flora Britannica*, states categorically (and wrongly) that it is native. Gooseberry was certainly in cultivation by 1275, but it took a long time to escape. Gerard, in his famous 1597 *Herball*, describes it as well-established in gardens, but said it had no name amongst old writers who either 'knew it not or esteemed it not'. It was not recorded in the wild until 1763.

Like many plants that have been cultivated for a very long time, the original native range of gooseberry is uncertain, although it's certainly European. But in a more recent twist to the gooseberry story, our plants probably now contain a few genes from significantly further afield. The reason is that in 1905 the European gooseberry faced a new and serious problem, when American gooseberry mildew (AGM) was accidentally introduced. European gooseberries have little resistance to this disease, and older susceptible varieties can be wiped out by it. I used to grow the old variety 'Leveller', until my bushes were basically killed by AGM.

Plant breeders quickly got to work incorporating resistance genes from four American species of *Ribes*, and there are now plenty of resistant cultivars available, although there is a suspicion that none taste quite as good as the old susceptible varieties.

But what about the poor old wild gooseberries? They were clobbered by AGM too, but studies suggest they have fought back by acquiring American resistance genes from their cultivated cousins. This can happen quite easily, since gooseberries are a favourite with bees, who can spread cultivated pollen far and wide. In fact wild gooseberries have become even more abundant in the last 50 years, probably owing to the continued escape of both resistant plants and resistant genes from gardens.

But I know what you're thinking; never mind AGM, has anyone found a gene that makes gooseberries resistant to gooseberry sawfly? Sadly, they haven't.

Bigger is better in the rain forest

Let's assume you would like your garden to have a 'tropical' look. What do you do? As everyone knows, tropical plants tend to have big leaves, so you grow the plants with the largest leaves you can find: *Musa*, cannas, palms, *Fatsia*, ferns etc.

But why do tropical plants have big leaves? To answer that question, you really ought to read a terrific recent paper in the journal *Science*, but I've saved you the trouble. The conventional wisdom, which is indeed entirely correct, is that big leaves are surrounded by a thicker 'boundary layer' of air that acts as a kind of blanket, reducing heat exchange with the surrounding air. Thus big leaves have trouble losing the heat they absorb from sunlight and run the risk of overheating, so in hot, sunny climates, leaves should be small.

But hold on a minute, didn't we just agree that tropical plants have big leaves? The key is plenty of water. Overheating is only really a problem if water is in short supply, since leaves can keep cool by transpiring lots of water. In classic tropical rain forest, water is not a problem and leaves can be as big as they like, keeping cool by transpiring gallons of water. So by going for big-leaved plants for the tropical look, you're effectively trying to simulate the hot, wet tropics.

So far so good, but that still doesn't explain why the

biggest leaves are in the tropics (which they undoubtedly are). Unlimited water may be crucial if big leaves are to avoid overheating, but there are plenty of wet (indeed very wet) places outside the tropics. Not only that, lower temperatures mean they don't have to worry so much about overheating, so why can't temperate plants have enormous leaves too?

To answer that question, you need to remember that leaves don't just get too *hot*, they can get too *cold* as well, especially at night, and here again leaf size is important. In cold climates leaves rapidly lose radiant heat to the nighttime sky, and to keep warm they need to absorb heat from the soil, the air and from other plants. But for big leaves, that pesky thick boundary layer reduces their ability to do this, making them susceptible to frost damage. The net result is that across the entire globe, the smallest leaves are found in hot, dry deserts and in cold, high-elevation regions such as Tibet and the Andes, but the reasons for their small leaves differ: shortage of water and danger of overheating in the former, and possible frost damage in the latter.

So, as a visit to the Palm House at Kew quickly demonstrates, big leaves are a reliable guide to the steamy-jungle look. In fact in the really wet bits of the tropics, temperature imposes no limit to leaf size, and the only thing that prevents the biggest leaves from being even bigger may be the difficulty of physically supporting them.

One final thing to remember is that although climate is certainly the dominant influence on *maximum* leaf size, that doesn't tell you how big the leaves of any individual species will be. Many other factors also play a part, so leaves are often smaller than the maximum permitted by the climate in any particular spot.

Nasty-smelling flowers

We grow flowers because they're pleasing to the human eye, and often because they smell nice too. Sometimes the smell is the main reason for growing a plant; it's hard to imagine that *Sarcococca*, say, would be widely grown if it wasn't pleasantly scented. The scents, of course, did not evolve to please you and me – they evolved to attract pollinators, overwhelmingly bees, but also butterflies and moths. It's therefore a massive stroke of good fortune for gardeners that bees and butterflies seem to like the same smells that we do. It doesn't have to be that way; bats, for example, tend to like smells that aren't entirely pleasant to a human nose.

Flower scents, of course, are not in themselves any kind of reward for a pollinating insect; they merely advertise the presence of the real reward, usually pollen or nectar. And, although there are cheats on both sides, plants at least are normally being honest with their pollinators: a pleasant scent does usually indicate the presence of something to eat.

There are, however, plants out there that are neither honest nor fragrant. These are plants that have evolved to deceive insects (often various kinds of flies) that lay their eggs in dung or carrion. The deceit is partly visual – there's not much point in being pink and fluffy if you're trying to attract an insect that's looking for a pile of poo. But research increasingly shows that the main deceit involves scent, for the simple reason that that's how the insects that exploit carrion and dung find their target. There is no shortage of such insects, because both dung and carrion are valuable, energy-rich resources, and there's a strong incentive to get to them before the competition.

According to a report in the journal *Ecology Letters*, the ability to smell like a corpse has evolved independently in at least five unrelated plant families. Some, like the huge-flowered parasitic *Rafflesia*, are entirely tropical. Others have names that leave very little to the imagination; you don't need me to tell you that you would probably be disappointed by the scent of *Helicodiceros muscivorus*, aka the dead-horse arum. The arum family has seriously embraced the idea of smelling horrible, often also using heat as an attractant. The enormous flower spikes of *Amorphophallus titanum*, the titan arum, can get up to 36°C. The heat probably serves the dual purpose of mimicking a freshly-dead animal, while also helping to spread the appalling smell of dead donkey.

Two of the key ingredients of the bad smell are dimethyl disulphide and dimethyl trisulphide. These two sulphur compounds are early breakdown products of proteins, specifically the sulphur-containing amino acids methionine and cysteine. Because they are released in the first stages of decomposition, they act as early warnings of a fresh corpse. They smell similar, and are often described as like rotting cabbage; they're also (and I really can't think of a polite way of putting this) one of the main reasons farts smell the way they do.

Not surprisingly, not many of these sorts of plants are all that popular with gardeners. One exception is pawpaw and its relatives (*Asimina* spp.). Pawpaw flowers have the classic brown/purple/red colour of flowers intended to mimic rotting flesh. They're sometimes described as smelling like rotting fish, but people seem to vary a lot in how sensitive they are to the smell. Another popular garden 'corpse flower' is *Eucomis bicolor*, although again opinions of its scent vary from 'awful' to merely 'slightly disagreeable'. I'm somewhere in the middle; to me, *Eucomis bicolor* is unpleasant, but there are (much) worse smells.

Plant killers give border guards the slip

We don't know exactly how ash dieback got into the UK. It's well dispersed by air, and it may well have made it here from Europe on its own. But even if it did, it almost certainly originally arrived from Asia with infected plants. Which all tends to concentrate minds on the role of horticulture in spreading plant pathogens around the globe.

One of the most insidious ways this can happen is via potted plants, either because the plants are infected, or because the pathogen is hiding in the soil, possibly in an inactive, quiescent state. To check how widespread this might be, Italian researchers looked for *Phytophthora* in potted plants from 'two large European retail nurseries' (they don't tell us who they were). Both nurseries, besides propagating native ornamentals, also import potted plants from outside the EU for propagation and resale, inside and outside Europe. The results were reported in the journal *Diversity and Distributions.*

The researchers chose *Phytophthora* because the various species cause a range of serious plant diseases, from potato blight to sudden oak death. But most infect roots, where they are effectively invisible until they cause symptoms serious enough to be seen above ground. Not only that, they may be present in soil as resting spores that can survive for a long time, and of course by definition don't provide any visible evidence of their presence, above or below ground. To get around this problem, the researchers developed a sensitive molecular probe that could identify *Phytophthora* DNA directly. They looked at seventeen widely-grown woody ornamentals, including box, Leyland cypress, hibiscus and cherry laurel.

Their results were – to me, anyway – startling. When carefully examined, a few plants showed symptoms of *Phytophthora*, and all these plants tested positive for *Phytophthora* DNA. But 70% of plants with no symptoms, either above or below ground, also tested positive. Nor was this entirely, or even mainly, because the pathogen was present as resting spores; in nearly half of the plants with no symptoms, *Phytophthora* was detected in root tissues. In other words, these plants were actually infected with *Phytophthora*. For good measure, the researchers also looked at samples of compost and irrigation water from the two nurseries. All water samples and a quarter of compost samples also tested positive for *Phytophthora*.

You don't need me to tell you that none of this is exactly reassuring. Some of the species found have numerous previous convictions; *P. cinnamomi* has already caused epidemics in Western Australia and on Mediterranean oaks, and although *P. cryptogea* was found only on cherry laurel, it can attack many widespread broadleaved trees.

Attempts to prevent the spread of pathogens in soil are certainly inadequate, and indeed are a nice demonstration of

144

wishful thinking in action. Because although the importation of soil itself into the EU is banned, the importation of plants growing in soil is not, as long as they have been officially declared free from harmful organisms. As the Italian research shows, any such declaration is hardly worth the paper it's written on. They must also show no sign of disease, but the sheer volume of trade means that few plants are inspected, and inspection reveals only the tip of the iceberg anyway. Once inside the EU, plants can be moved with very few restrictions, with or without soil. It would help if trade were limited to bare-root plants only, but recall that many plants with no symptoms nevertheless had infected roots; diseases aren't just in soil, they're in plants as well.

Will Brexit make any difference? Maybe, but don't hold your breath.

A volcanic surprise

Life, I often find myself thinking, is full of surprises, and by the end of this article we will have arrived at another of them. But let's start with the reasonable assumption that, all things being equal, the more sunshine plants receive, the faster they grow.

Just keep that in mind as I take you back to 15 June 1991 and the eruption of Mt Pinatubo in the Philippines. This was the second largest terrestrial eruption of the 20th century, ejecting about 10 cubic kilometres of magma and 20 million tons of sulphur dioxide into the atmosphere. It injected more dust and rubbish into the stratosphere than any eruption since Krakatoa.

You would expect something like that to have global effects, and it did, but the nature of those effects surprised everyone. Atmospheric CO_2 concentration, which had been rising inexorably (and still is), went into reverse for two years. This was particularly surprising since the eruption happened to coincide with an El Niño event, which is usually associated with an increase in atmospheric CO_2.

Scientists scrambled to find an explanation. Something was taking up more CO_2, but why, and where? Maybe it was something to do with changes in wind patterns over the Pacific ocean, or perhaps fertilisation of the ocean by iron ejected in the eruption? All that dust and (especially) sulphate aerosols also reduced global temperature by about 0.5°C, which should reduce the release of CO_2 by terrestrial respiration. But in the end, calculations showed that none of these effects was nearly big enough.

So what was going on? Pinatubo reduced the amount of sunlight reaching the earth's surface by a few percent, but its largest effect was a big reduction in direct sunlight, and a big increase in diffuse light. Why might that cause plants to grow faster, and take up more CO_2? Because, surprisingly, direct sunlight isn't all that good for plants. The average plant has several layers of leaves, so if you laid them all out side by side, they would cover five to ten times the area of ground occupied by the plant. In direct sunlight, the leaves at the top of the plant are brightly illuminated, but cast dense shade on all the leaves below, making the plant as a whole rather inefficient. Essentially the upper leaves have too much light, and all the rest don't have enough.

In diffuse light, where light comes at the plant from all angles, all the leaves get a fairer share of the light, so the plant grows faster. Nor do you need a volcanic eruption to show this. In a classic study in 1998, Australian researchers grew plants in full sun, and under two different kinds of shade. One type, using two layers of bird netting, reduced direct and diffuse light equally, while the other 'solarweave' shading reduced direct sunlight but increased diffuse light. Both reduced *total* light by exactly the same amount.

Under 'ordinary' shade, plant growth was reduced, as you might expect. But under the shade with an increased diffuse/direct ratio, plants grew bigger – in fact 18% bigger than plants in full sun, despite receiving only 75% of full sunlight. The researchers were able to work out that compared to full sun, the plants in diffuse shade were about 50% more efficient at turning the sun's energy into new growth.

Recent work has confirmed this finding in everything from trees to tomatoes.

Is all this of any practical use? Well, it certainly suggests that if you're buying material to cover a polytunnel, it's worth forking out for one that scatters a high proportion of the incident light, thus creating more diffuse lighting inside the tunnel. Outside, there's not much you can do to change the light environment, but maybe you don't need to, since you live in a country where the weather does most of the diffusing for you – the diffuse-light effect means that plants grow fastest with around 50% cloud cover.

The wrong watermelon

Carl Peter Thunberg was a Swedish naturalist and a pupil of the father of modern taxonomy, Carl Linnaeus. He is remembered in several plants familiar to gardeners, especially *Thunbergia alata* (black-eyed Susan) and *Berberis thunbergii*. In 1773, collecting plants in South Africa, he found and pressed a new plant that he named *Citrullus lanatus* or, to you and me, watermelon. The pressed specimen is still in the herbarium in Uppsala in Sweden.

Pressing specimens of plants in the family Cucurbitaceae

(gourds) isn't easy. The flowers and fruits are often large, fleshy, and difficult to preserve, and the leaves are often large and extremely variable. And Thunberg's specimen is a mess: just a few crumbly leaves that could be almost anything. Fortunately, modern taxonomists can look directly at DNA, which tells them exactly what a plant is, and what its closest relatives are. Two German botanists, in research reported in the journal *New Phytologist*, have done exactly that with Thunberg's plant.

So, is it a watermelon? No, it isn't. That is, it's not the same large, red-fleshed fruit that you or I can buy at any supermarket. Nor is it particularly closely related to that plant. Which is kind of a relief, because thinking that watermelons came from South Africa was starting to cause all kinds of problems. For a start, there are no wild watermelons in South Africa; as a wild plant, watermelons are endemic to west Africa. Furthermore, there's archaeological evidence of watermelons in south-west Libya about 5,000 years ago, and illustrations of watermelons in Egyptian tombs. No one has looked at the DNA of seeds found in ancient Egyptian tombs, including that of Tutankhamun, but they look suspiciously like watermelon too. None of this is consistent with watermelon, or its wild ancestor, being a South African plant.

So that leaves two questions. First, what is Thunberg's plant? It's actually *Citrullus amarus*, the citron melon. Its alternative names, preserving melon or jam melon, reflect the fact that it's rarely eaten raw, but has (apparently) been used for making jam for centuries. And if you've never heard of citron melon, you're not alone, I hadn't either and nor has anyone else as far as I can tell. My *New Oxford Book of Food Plants* mentions it not, there's no supplier in the RHS Plant Finder, and it may not even be in cultivation in the UK, so news of anyone who has tried growing it, or eaten the jam, would be welcome.*

Second, how did Thunberg come to think his plant was a watermelon? The answer is that he didn't. Linnaeus had described and named the true watermelon, which he called *Cucurbita citrullus*, twenty years earlier, and Thunberg knew his plant was a different species, which is why he gave it a different name. Thunberg's name only got mixed up with the watermelon in the 1930s, and the error spread until everyone believed the watermelon was *Citrullus lanatus*. Today, *C. lanatus* is so entrenched that the only realistic option is to consign the mix-up to the historical dustbin and accept that as the legitimate name for the watermelon.

---

* A lady in her eighties wrote to me to say that during the war and until the mid-1960s, her family bought melon jam from South Africa. It came in two-pound tins and was delicious. She later tried to make some but couldn't reproduce anything like it, and now thinks it must have been made from citron melon. A 60-year-old mystery solved!

That watermelons come from the wet tropics at least explains why most British gardeners find them not all that easy to grow, even in a greenhouse. If they really did originate from South Africa, they would probably need a bit less heat, and maybe a bit less water too. Musk or cantaloupe melons (*Cucumis melo*), which British gardeners generally find more accommodating, come from Iran and neighbouring countries. In fact the entire gourd family are plants of warm climates, barely making it into Britain; our one native species, white bryony (*Bryonia dioica*), is common only in the warmer and drier parts of England, and is more or less absent from Wales and Scotland.

Ecology at Chelsea 2017

The British Ecological Society (BES), the world's oldest ecological society, is back in the discovery zone at Chelsea, and this time the focus is on something many gardeners struggle with: shade, and what to grow in it.

The first thing to notice is that many of the plants we see in shady places aren't really shade-tolerant at all, instead they're shade *avoiders*. So 'vernals' like daffodils and bluebells exploit the brief window between winter and the closing of the tree canopy, fitting most of their growing and flowering into the key months of March–May. Foxgloves, on the other hand, have tiny seeds that can survive in woodland soil for at least 100 years, waiting for a natural or man-made gap in the canopy. The young foxgloves grow rapidly and produce a large rosette in the first year, then flower, seed and die in the second year. This biennial strategy turns out to be the optimum one for exploiting the brief window of opportunity presented by short-lived gaps in woodland.

But what about *real* shade plants, those that can survive and even thrive in continuous shade? Here natural selection has come up with a variety of interesting solutions, but one thing is constant: being short of light means being short of carbon, so all genuinely shade-tolerant plants are slow-growing. Many are tough too, since being unable to grow your way out of trouble makes it doubly important to try to avoid being eaten in the first place. Classic native examples, also frequently found in gardens, are butcher's broom (*Ruscus aculeatus*), stinking flag (*Iris foetidissima*) and spurge laurel (*Daphne laureola*).

In the gloom of the forest floor, light may be up to ten million times fainter than in the open; not only that, it's had the wavelengths plants normally use for photosynthesis taken out by the trees above. Mostly what's left is green, which isn't much use. This desperate situation calls for desperate measures, and some plants of deep shade, such as

152

some begonias, have leaves with a strange blue iridescence, but research has only just revealed what this does.

Iridescent plants have evolved specially-modified chloroplasts, called iridoplasts. Iridoplasts can actually slow light down (don't ask how; the answer made my head hurt), plus they're much better at using green light. A side-effect is reflection of blue light, giving the leaves their iridescence, but this doesn't matter on the forest floor where there is much more green light than blue light. The net result is an improvement in the efficiency of photosynthesis under low light by 5 to 10%, which may not sound like much, but it gives them an edge in deep shade.

Where light is desperately short, brief shafts of sunlight, or *sunflecks*, are priceless. But sunflecks can be perilous; in plants accustomed to dim light, such sudden exposure to bright light might actually damage the photosynthetic machinery. One answer is structural variegation: air spaces inside the leaf, resulting in a characteristic silvery variegation. The air gap bounces light around inside the leaf, scattering light from the sunfleck over a wider area, reducing the possibility of damage and giving all parts of the leaf a share. Good examples in the garden are pulmonarias, *Brunnera* 'Jack Frost' and many large-leaved begonias.

Finally, what about the famous shade-tolerance of ferns? Part of this ability stems from a unique light-sensing chemical called *neochrome* that enables ferns to detect and respond to all the wavelengths of light available under tree canopies (other plants can detect only one – blue or red). But where did ferns get neochrome from? Research published only in 2013 reveals that they stole the gene for making it from hornworts, little-known cousins of mosses and liverworts, about 180 million years ago. Once they got their hands on neochrome ferns never looked back, and their unique ability is one reason they're the dominant plants of forest floors across the globe.

The BES exhibit will have a hornwort for you to look at, but I suspect few will go away with the urge to grow one.

Twigs laid bare

It's not every day you open a book that genuinely expands your horizons, but that's what happened when I opened my new copy of John Poland's *Field Key to Winter Twigs*. Let's be honest, winter can be a dull time for the gardener; there's a limit to the amount of time you can spend reading seed catalogues. But here is a whole new winter activity that hardly involves going outside at all, and can mostly be carried out in an armchair in front of the fire, cup of tea and chocolate biscuit at your elbow.

All you need is some young twigs, a decent hand lens and a ruler, and you're ready to sort out all those annoying trees and shrubs in the local park or road verges. OK, I know there's nothing to stop you doing that in the summer, using the more traditional flowers, leaves etc., but there always seems to be something better to do in the summer, and it turns out that bare twigs are surprisingly informative.

There's quite a bit of botanical detail to cope with, so full marks for Poland's attempts to come up with some memorable images to help us on our way. Like the 'hula skirt' papery sheath at the base of Japanese maple buds, or the sharply curved up and down lower branches of horse chestnut. 'Like an elephant's trunk – imagination required!' says Poland, and I can see what he means on both counts. As for the 'monkey-face' leaf scars of walnuts, the description is spot on – once seen, never forgotten.

Even so, I admit you have to learn quite a bit of new jargon, and you also have to accept that some familiar words have precise botanical meanings that you ignore at your peril. How many of us, for example, have ever given much thought to the difference between prickles, spines and thorns? Not many, and maybe you'd still be happy not to, but I'm going to enlighten you anyway.

Prickles are simply an extension of the plant's skin, or epidermis, and can occur anywhere on a twig or branch.

Roses and brambles are the classic examples. Spines are modified leaves or stipules (bracts, sometimes very leaf-like, found on the petiole (leaf stalk), or on the twig at the base of the petiole). In either case, spines occur directly *below* a leaf scar or a bud since buds are always in the angle between leaf and stem. Robinia, berberis and gooseberry (and cacti of course) all have spines. Thorns, on the other hand, are modified branches and therefore always occur *above* a leaf scar or at the end of a short branch. Thorns can terminate the main twig or a side twig and (because they're branches) they can bear buds and leaf scars of their own.

Contrary to the normal dictates of sod's law, buckthorn, hawthorn and blackthorn really do have thorns, and neither prickles nor spines (so whoever named blackthorn *Prunus spinosa* was having a laugh).

Since roses don't have thorns, does that mean 'a rose between two thorns' is wrong? I don't think so; the allusion is surely to the plant rather than the flower, so it's a rose (-bush) between two thorn (-bushes).

Two royal flowers

The Queen's annual trip to Chelsea notwithstanding, it's not often that the combination of royalty and gardening is headline news, but I couldn't help noticing the botanical aspects of Meghan Markle's new coat of arms. Specifically, as a palace spokesman said, 'Beneath the shield on the grass sits a collection of golden poppies, California's state flower, and wintersweet, which grows at Kensington Palace.'

Two pretty, garden-worthy plants there, especially Californian poppy (*Eschscholzia californica*), a cheerful annual that most of us will have grown at some time or other. For a dry, sunny spot, it's hard to beat, and although poppies don't produce nectar, they're a great source of pollen for bees.

But wintersweet? Wintersweet (*Chimonanthus praecox*) is one of the very best winter-flowering shrubs, with an extremely sweet, penetrating scent. A plant many of us would be happy to have on our coat of arms. But I've no doubt there are plenty of other lovely plants in the garden at Kensington Palace, so why pick on that? The romantic in me imagined the delightful scent in the background of one of Harry and Meghan's early meetings, their first kiss, maybe?

Meghan: 'What's that beautiful smell, darling?'

Harry: 'Search me, ask the gardener.'

Or something like that, anyway. But in fact the timing is all wrong. Harry and Meghan met on a blind date in early July 2016, and news of their relationship became public in late October. So by the time they had an opportunity for a joint sniff of wintersweet, in the following winter, the early days of the romance were over.

So why Meghan chose wintersweet will remain a mystery, at least to me. But if you want to follow in the royal footsteps and grow it, what do you need to know? Like many winter-flowering shrubs (including my favourite, *Lonicera fragrantissima*), it's really rather dull for most of the year and a bit big too, ten feet or more tall and the same wide, so not a plant for those pushed for space. If you do have room, I would make sure it's planted near a door, where you will pass it in the winter without having to make a special, muddy expedition to the bottom of the garden. In fact the smell is so strong that you'll probably smell it wherever it is, but the flowers are worth a close look, with an outer set of thin, almost translucent, pale yellow petals, and an inner set streaked with reddish-purple.

Does the plant in the coat of arms look much like wintersweet? No, not really, and apart from clearly being borne on leafless stems, the flowers could be almost anything. And *Eschscholzia* and *Chimonanthus* in flower at the same time is pure artistic licence, but I guess you can do what you like on a coat of arms.

Turning sunflowers

As every schoolboy knows, sunflowers turn to follow the sun as it moves across the sky. Or do they? Plenty of people must think so, because some of the sunflower's names in other languages refer directly to this behaviour, e.g. *gira-sol* and *tournesol*. Yet Gerard, in his famous 1597 *Herball*, was having none of it: 'some have reported it to turn with the sun, the which I could never observe, although I have endeavoured to find out the truth of it.' We now think we know why Gerard was confused; only immature sunflower heads follow the sun. Once the flowers mature and start to shed pollen, they settle down and face east for the rest of their lives. But others were confused too, and the sunflower's daily rotation was only finally established beyond doubt (with photographs) in the 1890s.

But that's only the start; why do they do it? A recent paper in the journal *Plant Science* looked at the evidence, and frankly, no one really knows, although there's no short-age of hypotheses. For example, plenty of plants (including sunflowers) have leaves that follow the sun, and such behav-iour definitely increases photosynthesis. So flower turning may just be an accidental side-effect of changing orientation of the leaves, or maybe even of the photosynthetic bracts beneath the head itself.

Or the main reason may be the maintenance of a higher and more constant temperature, perhaps helping to attract more pollinators or speed up seed development. But when rotation stops, why do sunflowers always end up facing east? Again, there are somewhat contradictory hypotheses. Maybe facing east in the morning dries out the morning dew and reduces the possibility of fungal infection. Or maybe, possibly like the rotation itself, more rapid warming in the morning is all about attracting more pollinators. Alternatively, perhaps facing east helps to keep the flower *cool* on hot afternoons (pollen grains in particular don't like to be too hot).

One problem is that most researchers have studied sunflowers cultivated for oil or for ornament, but the turning behaviour presumably evolved in their wild ancestors, which are very different plants, much more branched and with much smaller flowers. Maybe we need to pay more attention to these wild ancestors.

When it comes to the how rather than why, we know a bit more; for a start, a moving light source is essential. Sunflowers don't turn if you raise them in a room with stationary, overhead lighting. But at least part of the daily cycle doesn't need light, because sunflowers turn back to face east at night, and in fact this movement is about twice

160

as fast as the daytime motion. And once they get started, sunflowers tend to stick with the same routine. If you confuse a sunflower by rotating it through 180° at night, it carries on regardless, only re-coordinating with the sun after several days of facing the wrong way. It also doesn't look like the flower itself is all that important; if you decapitate a sunflower, the stump continues to turn. But leaves *are* necessary – remove them and movement stops. Not just any old leaves, either; movement ceases if you remove the mature leaves, but starts again when young leaves reach maturity.

But what is a sunflower doing as it turns? Well, one thing it isn't doing is actually turning; all that happens is that the shaded side of the stem below the head grows faster than the illuminated side. So rather than rotating, the flower is better described as tilting towards the sun. Which helps to explain why movement ceases when the flower head is mature and growth stops.

Clearly we're still several PhD theses away from fully understanding why sunflowers behave the way they do. In the meantime, it seems to me that trying to grow the tallest example in the neighbourhood is one of the least interesting things about sunflowers.

PRACTICAL
GARDENING

Christmas tree care

If you were starting to worry that scientists never do anything useful, here's some genuinely worthwhile research: how to look after your Christmas tree. It was published nearly two years ago, but I missed it at the time and, as far as I can tell, so did almost everyone else. One reason may be that it was published in the *Australian Journal of Botany*, not a journal I normally associate with Christmas. It was also first published online on 5 February 2016, and I suspect that if you wanted to smuggle out some Christmas-related research at the time it would attract the least attention, the first week of February would be a good bet.

The tree in question is Monterey pine, *Pinus radiata*. Which is fair enough; for me, *the* Christmas tree is Norway spruce (even though most people now go for Nordmann fir), but neither is easy to come by in Australia. Anyway, I suspect that when it comes to what happens when you cut down a tree and put it in a bucket of water in your front room, one evergreen conifer behaves much like another.

The researchers tested four treatments that have been suggested to prolong the health of cut trees. First, spraying the foliage with hairspray; water loss is the big problem for cut trees, and hairspray should reduce that by blocking the stomata. Second, energy drink, because the sugar in the drink might give the plants energy. Previous research has shown that cut flowers last longer in sugar solution than in pure water. Third, freshly boiled (i.e. still hot) water, in the hope that this would dissolve the sticky sap at the end of the cut stem and improve water uptake (of course the water quickly cools to room temperature). Fourth, beer (diluted 50/50 with water), because there's plenty around at Christmas and, a bit like the energy drink, it contains lots of nutrients and minerals that might feed the tree. The alcohol might also kill any germs. Finally, plain cold tap water as a control (also used for the hairspray-treated trees).

The trees were kept under typical 'room' conditions for a month and needle health was monitored using a chlorophyll fluorescence meter. That may sound complicated, but it corresponded closely to a visual estimation of health, i.e. the trees with the best objectively-measured health also looked the best.

So what did they find? Beer and energy drink were easily the worst, although the possibility remains that a more dilute solution of either might do better. Water, either cold or boiled, was better. But best of all was hairspray. Needles on hairspray-treated trees were as healthy after a month as they were at the start, and the trees were even starting to show new growth. So hairspray wins hands down, although it's highly flammable, so the injunction to keep your tree away from naked flames applies even more than usual (maybe less of a problem in Australia, unless your tree is too near the barbie).

Finally, two other tips that are slightly more use here than Australia. Your tree will last longer in a cool room, or at least not next to a central heating radiator. And trees stay healthy longer if they're harvested after experiencing some cold weather (say around 5°C), so buy a freshly-harvested tree, as near Christmas as possible.

Saving the world, one bag of compost at a time

So the Committee on Climate Change has spoken. And what they say is that we can achieve zero carbon emissions by 2050, but we need to make a few changes in our lives. Some are simple, and will make us healthier and save us money, as well as helping to save the planet: for example, walk, cycle or take public transport rather than drive, and eat less beef, lamb and dairy. Others are a bit more challenging, such as buying an electric car and flying less, especially long-haul.

But right in the middle of the Committee's shopping list is something really simple, something many of you will have done already, and if you haven't, you can resolve to do it right now, this minute: use only peat-free compost.

Why focus on peat and climate change? The Committee know that as well as producing less CO_2, we need to improve the ability of the natural world to absorb CO_2, so they say we need to grow more trees – *lots* more trees. But they are also aware that most of the world's terrestrial, organic carbon resides not in plants and trees, but in soil. There's about four times more carbon in soils than in vegetation, and most of that is in peat. Which is why another plank of their suggested strategy is to manage our peatlands better and to restore degraded peatlands. That's actually quite hard work, but surely a good start would be to leave our existing peat where it is, rather than digging it up and flogging it to gardeners.

Because once peat is extracted, it's only a matter of time before it is returned to the atmosphere as CO_2. Not only that, the bogs from which the peat is taken are damaged, and sometimes destroyed completely; quite apart from the loss of their unique biodiversity, they would have done more to help in the fight against climate change if we'd left them alone. And given that there's absolutely no need to make compost from peat, why not do that?

Peat-free composts have gained a reputation for being a bit unreliable, and sometimes not very good at all. But the only reason for that is that many contain green waste, which is very variable in composition and not very stable, so it tends to continue to decompose once it's turned into compost. The best peat-free composts don't use green waste at all. My favourite brand is Melcourt Sylvagrow, which is made from coniferous bark, wood fibre (both by-products of sustainably managed British forests) and coir.

I've no interest in trying to persuade you to buy any particular brand, and other good peat-free composts are available, but Sylvagrow happens to be the one I use, and I've always had excellent results. Not only that, last year I visited Thornhayes nursery in Devon and talked to its owner, Kevin Croucher. Kevin has been growing quality trees and shrubs since 1991, and he told me that Melcourt composts were not only the best peat-free composts he had ever used, they were the best composts of *any* kind that he had ever used.

So next time you're buying compost, ignore the cheap three-bags-for-the-price-of-two peat-based variety, and instead buy a quality (green waste-free) peat-free compost. If your local garden centre doesn't stock such a thing, tell them it's time they did, and then go elsewhere.

We are all permaculturists now

Some time ago now, I wrote an article that was mildly critical of permaculture. In fact not so much critical as puzzled, because in truth, I couldn't figure out what permaculture is supposed to be. In the end, I got the impression that forest gardening and permaculture are at least distant cousins, so I contented myself with observing that forest gardening may have many virtues, but a sensible way of growing food isn't one of them.

But it continued to bother me that I still don't understand what permaculture is all about. I carefully read one blogger's attempt to enlighten me. I even went so far as to buy – and read – a book on permaculture. None of this helped; permaculture remained a curious mixture of the prosaic and the wacky, with no obvious unifying principles (at least, not obvious to me).

But, reading a scientific paper the other day, I had an epiphany. The paper, in the journal *Acta Horticulturae*, has three French authors – two academics and a farmer. It asks an interesting question: is it possible for a single market gardener, 'inspired by permaculture principles', to make an acceptable income from a small acreage, cultivated without powered machinery?

The answer to that question isn't strictly part of our story, but it's worth reporting. Basically, yes. A single market gardener, working 43 hours per week, could make a living from 6 hectares of land, selling produce direct to consumers and restaurants. But there are two important caveats. First, 40% of the cultivated area was under glass, but that generated 64% of the income; in other words, a large area under glass is essential. Second, a decent income relied mainly on short-cycle crops such as leafy vegetables and fruit with a high added value. Potatoes take up too much space, for too long; if customers wanted potatoes, they had to be imported from a local organic farmer who *did* use machinery.

But back to the main story. What are these principles inspired by permaculture? Helpfully, the paper lists them:

Growing more per unit area: making best use of the microclimate, high crop density, continuous rotation of short-cycle crops, relay-cropping, high level of care given to crops, extending growing season under glass.

Limiting material inputs: no expensive powered machinery, recycling nutrients inside the site (i.e. composting), use of local organic waste.

Reducing workload: less weeding through high crop density and multi-cropping, limiting soil tillage and using efficient manual tools.

Now, I don't know about you, but my first thought on looking at that list was: 'that looks a lot like gardening'. Or at any rate, even if I don't always succeed, the way I try to garden the 'productive' part of my garden. Or to put it very simply: *permaculture is gardening.* Which isn't surprising when you consider that permaculture started out as an enlightened approach to farming – essentially trying to get farmers to behave a bit more like gardeners.

As many people have pointed out, gardening is inherently both more sustainable and more productive than farming. So as long as you're a careful, thoughtful sort of gardener, composting all your waste, trying to make sure every bit of ground always has something growing in it, and going easy on wasteful and expensive machinery and chemicals, you're probably doing most of what permaculture involves already. On the other hand, if you can't imagine gardening without neonicotinoids, glyphosate and the internal combustion engine, maybe permaculture isn't for you.

Beware of fuchsia gall mite

One of the less welcome consequences of my now not-so-recent move to Devon was making the acquaintance of a pest that I'd not previously heard of: fuchsia gall mite. For those of you who know it, fuchsia gall mite will need no introduction. For the rest of you, it's a tiny mite that infests the new growth of fuchsias, sucking the sap and secreting chemicals that cause the foliage and flowers to become increasingly distorted and enlarged. In severe cases the plants no longer produce normal leaves or flower buds, and growth consists of a mass of distorted tissue.

Fuchsia gall mite comes from South America, and is living proof that unauthorised movement of plants across borders can be a really bad idea. No one knows how the mite first got to California, where it was first found in 1981, but its subsequent arrival in France and Germany is thought to have been amateur gardeners (illegally) importing infested cuttings from the USA. Mites in the UK, where it was first reported in 2007, may have come directly from South America, or Europe, or the Channel Islands; no one knows, but once again human agency is suspected.

At present the mite is much more common in the south, which is why I had never seen it before. Evidence about its climatic tolerances is a bit contradictory. In California it's reported to tolerate temperatures down to 5°C, but I've seen it here in Devon in 2018, so it clearly survived the 'Beast from the East', which was much colder than that. In any case, it's recently been reported from Stockport and Lincolnshire, so there seems no reason why it shouldn't eventually colonise the whole of England and Wales at least.

The good news is that some fuchsias are more resistant

than others. The bad news is that most common species and varieties are susceptible, including the ubiquitous and hardy *Fuchsia magellanica*. Resistant species *F. microphylla*, *F. thymifolia* and *F. arborescens* have small flowers or are not very hardy, but at least suggest that fuchsia breeders have some resistance to work with, and might – eventually – be able to breed resistant larger-flowered, hardy varieties.

My experience? Several fuchsias that I inherited in my new garden were badly infested, and a fuchsia I had brought with me rapidly succumbed. There is no chemical control, and simply cutting out the obviously infected shoots was a waste of time. So I tried cutting my fuchsias right down to the ground, but new growth the following season was still infested. I then dug them out completely, but some have come back from fragments of root left in the ground. This new growth, touch wood, is clear.*

What should you do? I don't think I can improve on the advice from the British Fuchsia Society:

✐ Be careful about where you get your fuchsias from and be on the lookout for plants with symptoms. Learn what the early signs look like.

---

* I spoke too soon – the mite is still there. Instant removal of any shoot showing the first signs of infection is (just) keeping it at bay for the moment, but I fear this is a battle I'm destined to lose.

- Don't take cuttings of fuchsias from the wild or in public areas. If offered a cutting think twice and have a look around at all their plants for any signs of damage.

- Only buy from sources, including mail order, that you can be sure of. If buying from a nursery, look around and check for gall mite damage before purchasing any plants.

- Don't bring back fuchsia cuttings from Europe or the Channel Islands.

- Check your plants weekly during the growing season.

- Without intruding, keep an eye on your neighbours' fuchsias and don't be shy of telling them if you spot symptoms. If this seems nosy, just remember that if a neighbour gets it and you do nothing, then you will get it too and so will everyone else.

For the best meadow, sow the best seeds

Growing wildflowers has never been more popular, and the cheapest way to do it is to start from seed. But there's always been a bit of a question mark over the quality of commercial wildflower seeds, so I was interested to read a report of a recent EU-funded project that looked at the quality of the seeds of eight wildflowers, bought from 24 seed suppliers from right across Europe, from Sweden to Italy and Spain. The results were published in the journal *Seed Science and Technology*. The researchers also checked the purity of all eight species, i.e. how many of the seeds were what they claimed to be. The news here was generally good; in most samples purity was above 90%, and the percentage of contaminating species was less than 1% in over half the samples.

But the purity of *Rhinanthus minor*, yellow rattle, was unusually poor. Some samples were good, but some were not, and in one sample more than half the seeds were contaminants. What were these contaminants, you may well ask? A ragbag of buttercups, plantains, docks, forget-me-nots and campions, plus various grasses. Given that yellow rattle has very distinctive, large seeds, it's clear that some of these samples had been subject to no quality control at all – the most cursory inspection would have shown that they were not all they claimed to be. And especially for yellow rattle, quality control really is crucial. Because it's a hemiparasite, it can't (even theoretically) be grown on its own, so careless harvesting is always going to produce a mixture of seeds of various species.

When it comes to germination, some samples of all eight species were very poor, with low or even zero viability (and hence germination). The common corn poppy was especially bad, with many very poor samples, and even the best managing only about 60% germination. But once again the species that stood out was yellow rattle. Some samples were really good, but many were not, and in three out of seventeen samples, all the seeds were dead.

We don't know why yellow rattle viability was so poor, but it turns out that harvesting has a bearing on seed quality. In four species it was possible to compare samples from multiple hand harvests with those from a single mechanical harvest. The former were consistently better, sometimes dramatically so, although it's not possible to pin down precisely why. Multiple hand harvests may just produce better seeds, perhaps because mature seeds are actively selected. But it's also possible that seeds were damaged by the process of mechanical harvesting itself. Whatever the cause, it looks like you get what you pay for: the expensive, hand-harvesting option produces better seeds.

When we're all being advised to add yellow rattle to wildflower meadows to help control the vigour of grasses, it's clear that the quality of commercial seeds is unacceptable. One option, which I adopted when I established yellow rattle in a meadow in my old garden, is to collect your own from the wild. You don't need many seeds for this; yellow rattle is an annual, and as long as it's happy in your meadow, the size of your yellow rattle population will very soon be determined by the number of seeds produced the previous year, and not by the number you started out with.

Finally, always remember that yellow rattle seeds need a long period of cold to break dormancy, so always sow them as soon as they're ripe. And don't cut your meadow until the ripe yellow rattle seeds have been shed.

Conflicting tomato advice

It's always tempting, as the summer wears on, to remove the tatty lower leaves on vegetables where the harvested part is fruit (rather than leaves, say). I'm thinking particularly here of tomatoes. The RHS isn't sure whether this is a good idea or not, and hedges its bets on different parts of its website. In its grow-your-own pages advice is clear: 'Remove yellowing leaves below developing fruit trusses.' The Hessayon *Vegetable and Herb Expert* says much the same: 'Remove yellowing leaves below fruit trusses as the season progresses', but adds a note of caution: '… but never overdo this deleafing process.'

The RHS tomato profile page is even more cautious: 'Leaves below the lowest truss still bearing fruit can be removed to help control disease. However, de-leafing is best avoided.' It's not clear which diseases might be controlled by removing lower leaves, nor why the RHS think this might sometimes not be a good idea.* So what does the research say? There's plenty of it, because tomatoes are such an important crop, and people have long been interested in what happens if you remove the lower leaves.

One old study simply divided the leaf canopy up into three layers of equal depth, then removed them in turn from the bottom up to see what happened. The results were clear: the lower leaves of a tomato plant don't do much. Even though the lowest layer had the largest area, removing it had a negligible effect on total photosynthesis. The top layer, on the other hand, although less than a quarter of the leaf area, accounted for two-thirds of total photosynthesis.

Studies in other crops show much the same; in sweet peppers, removing the entire bottom half of the leaf canopy had no effect on yield. This is partly due to the lower efficiency of old leaves, and partly because the upper leaves intercept most of the light. What's more, although the RHS advice is only about leaves *below* the lowest fruit truss, other evidence suggests that going a bit further might be a good idea. In another study, when leaves were removed up to

---

* The RHS revised its tomato-growing advice after I wrote this column, so at least the different parts of its website now give the same advice.

two trusses *above* the ripening truss, fruits were warmer and ripened earlier than those on plants where only lower leaves were removed. Nor did this have any effect on yield.

Recently, researchers have even entertained the idea that removing a few *young* leaves might not be a bad idea. The theory is that the loss of leaf area is only small, and the plant is thus persuaded to allocate resources to developing fruit rather than to growing new leaves. Unfortunately, results so far show that the loss of even a few efficient young leaves reduces yield, even if only a bit, so this doesn't look like a good idea.

But all the evidence suggests that removing old leaves certainly doesn't do any harm, and may even have benefits. And note that this research was all about yield and fruit ripening; if removing leaves reduces disease as well, that's just a bonus.

It's worth noting that all this research was carried out, not surprisingly, with the needs of commercial growers in mind. Those commercial growers normally grow indeterminate (cordon) varieties. Not only that, they also tend to grow very tall cordons with many more trusses of fruit than us amateurs ever manage (or have room for). This is one reason the lower leaves are so useless – the taller the cordon, the darker it is at the bottom. To overcome this, researchers have even experimented with providing extra light inside the canopy, as well as the normal top light.

With bush varieties, which grow sideways rather than upwards, there's less shading of old leaves by new ones, so the argument for removing old leaves is weaker. In Sheffield, where it was only worth growing tomatoes in a greenhouse, I usually grew 'Gardener's Delight'. But I'm just coming to the end of my first tomato season in Devon, and I've had spectacular success with bush variety 'Tumbler' grown outdoors; in fact, I'm rapidly running out of tomato recipes.

Cures for weeds in paving

Weeds in paving are annoying, aren't they? In fact because it's supposed to be one of the tidiest bits of the garden, weedy paving somehow seems more offensive – and maybe more noticeable too – than weeds elsewhere in the garden. And although weeds in paving are easy enough to control with herbicides, an increasing number of gardeners don't like to use them. Official interest in non-chemical control has been stimulated by the European Water Framework Directive, which aims to reduce pesticide residues in water. The Flemish government has agreed to phase out completely the use of herbicides on public pavements, so the search for 'green' alternatives is urgent. A major Belgian research project, reported in the journal *Weed Research*, has some useful lessons for gardeners.

First of all, not all paving materials are the same. Pavers made of porous material allow water to drain away from the surface, and this lack of surface water strongly inhibits germination and growth of weeds. So, all things being equal, porous pavers are much the best material for reducing weed problems. Unfortunately, this lack of water doesn't much bother mosses, but most people consider moss less offensive than larger weeds. For the same reason, pavers laid on a coarse, free-draining bedding layer are less weedy than those laid on finer, less permeable material.

Joints between pavers should be narrow, but don't assume that what you fill them with doesn't matter. Compared to ordinary sand, a special sand enriched with sodium silicate drastically reduced weed growth; in fact, as long as it remained reasonably free of organic dirt and dust, the enriched sand more or less completely prevented weed germination and growth. The cause is excess sodium, which increases the osmotic pressure of the soil water, preventing seeds and roots from absorbing water and effectively killing emerging seedlings by drought. The brand the researchers used was Dansand®, which is widely available in the UK. But it is expensive; sea sand is a much cheaper but less effective alternative (but still better than ordinary sand).

But eventually you'll still get some weeds, so how do

you kill them? The clear winner among brushing, hot water, hot air and flaming was hot water, with significantly fewer treatments required to maintain an acceptably weed-free state than with other methods. The Belgian researchers had a fancy self-propelled machine that detected weeds and then squirted them with almost boiling (98°C) water, but there doesn't appear to be a domestic equivalent. However, there's nothing to stop you using a kettle, but wear suitable footwear and gloves to protect you from steam; gardens are dangerous enough places already, without adding another source of avoidable injury.

The researchers also found that to some extent, susceptibility to control methods is species-specific; different methods work best on different weeds. So even if you settle on a particular treatment that works for you, the optimum strategy is to occasionally throw in a different treatment, to prevent a build-up of whichever weeds happen to be most tolerant of your chosen method.

A final thing to bear in mind is the importance of cleanliness. The effectiveness of any weed-control strategy is reduced as the joints fill up with organic muck, and even Dansand, completely weed-proof when reasonably clean, eventually allows some weed growth. Don't underestimate the preventive powers of the regular application of a good stiff broom.

Preparing for climate change

When screenwriter William Goldman famously said 'nobody knows anything', he was talking about the inability of anyone in Hollywood to predict what would turn out to be the next blockbuster. But he might have been talking about gardening and climate change, where no one seems to know for sure what to expect, or how to prepare for it.

So I was intrigued to see a report of a project by the Royal Botanic Garden Edinburgh, attempting to answer just that question. Edinburgh and its three regional outposts (Edinburgh is the driest, Dawyck the coldest, Benmore the wettest and Logan the mildest) have plenty of interesting weather between them, so they're in a good position to see what needs to be done, and what works and what doesn't.

The project assumed that although no one can predict the future, it's a safe bet that there will be more extreme weather of every kind. So they asked: what have we learned from recent extreme weather, which has included both drought and the wettest year on record, some of the warmest *and* coldest winters in living memory, and hurricane-force winds. Naturally, some of the lessons learned apply only to large public gardens, but some have wider relevance. For example, a storm in January 2012 broke over 600 panes of glass in various glasshouses, so Edinburgh has decided to keep much larger stocks of replacement glass, enabling repairs to be made much more quickly.

You and I are never going to have storm damage on that scale, but it would still pay to have a couple of spare panes in case of breakage. Edinburgh has also adopted a zero-tolerance approach to cracked or loose panes and other glasshouse problems that might make them less wind-resistant, which is something we could usefully emulate. Nor does that apply only to greenhouses; checking the state of gutters and tiles and the health of any large trees isn't a bad idea either.

On the subject of wind, Edinburgh also found that some large-leaved evergreens, particularly rhododendrons, suffered badly from wind rock. In future they will take care that new plants are sited in the most sheltered places, and that windbreaks are erected or grown to protect existing plantings. We should probably be doing the same.

Hotter, drier summers mean it wouldn't do any harm to store more water, so if you don't have a water butt, why not? If you already have one, why not get another? And a good thick mulch is always a good idea; it will both retain soil moisture in dry weather and protect soil from heavy rain. The prospect of drier summers has also persuaded

Edinburgh to relocate humidity-loving, large-leaved rhododendrons to (wetter) Benmore. Obviously we can't do
that, but unless you garden somewhere that's not only wet,
but forecast to stay that way, maybe you should think twice
about trying to grow moisture-loving plants at all.

But of all the problems faced by Edinburgh and its
regional gardens, mild, wet winters may have been the
worst. One response has been a regular regime of main-
taining existing, and installing new, drains and soakaways,
along with replacement of concrete or tarmac paths with
porous paving such as gravel. All this helps to avoid both
waterlogging, slippery paths and soil compaction.

Gardeners often worry about the effect of dry summers
on lawns, but grass will recover from all but the most severe
drought. Wet weather, often coupled with warm winters,
may be a bigger problem. Wet weather makes grass grow
faster, and warmer winters may mean that grass grows
almost all year round. In turn this means more mowing,
but saturated ground may make mowing difficult or even
impossible. In future, those in wetter parts of the country,
or on clay soils, might want to think carefully about how
much lawn they really need, or even whether to have any
at all. And grass paths, attractive as they are, may have to
go for the same reason; both Edinburgh and Dawyck have
replaced grass (and bark) paths with gravel.

Mild winters will also increase the risk of pests and

diseases, and some glasshouse pests may even move outdoors. But that's another story.

Plants to cope with flooding

As you will have noticed, many of us had yet another wet winter; hardly surprising, since this is what models of climate change have been predicting for years. But if this is going to keep happening, and I think we can assume it is, then it presents gardeners with some difficult questions. Basically, what should we be growing that will thrive (or at least, survive) under the new conditions?

It's tempting to reach for plants that grow in wet (or at least damp) places, and thus with a proven ability to survive waterlogging. But the drawback with that approach is that another climate change prediction is higher temperatures and lower rainfall in summer; conditions that are unlikely to please plants of moist soils. I know this to my cost. My old garden in Sheffield, perhaps because it was on the side of a hill, was basically quite well-drained, but that didn't stop me trying to grow plants of damp soils. Over the years, *Tropaeolum speciosum*, *Primula florindae*, *Camassia leichtlinii* and *Monarda didyma* among others all arrived, malingered for a while and then expired, essentially for lack of a good drink.

But if we grow plants that we know can survive drought, will they keel over the first winter they find themselves up to their necks in water? A question that prompted researchers at the Universities of Reading and Sheffield to do some experiments; the results were published a few years ago in the journal *Landscape and Urban Planning*.

The plants they chose to study were *Stachys byzantina* (lambs' ears), *Cistus* × *hybridus* (white rock rose), *Lavandula angustifolia* (English lavender) and *Salvia officinalis* (sage). These are all Mediterranean 'garrigue' plants, more than capable of putting up with as much drought as they are ever likely to experience in Britain, whatever the ravages of climate change. But how do they enjoy a good British soak?

To find out, the researchers subjected them to a variety of climatic ordeals, both in a greenhouse and in the garden. In one experiment, they were grown on the flood plain of the River Wey at Wisley in Surrey, which involved three weeks of continuous saturation in February and March. In another, plants in pots were exposed to water up to the top of the compost for up to seventeen days, at three different times of year.

The results were surprising. In some species, a few plants died and growth of the survivors was reduced if flooding occurred in spring or summer, but all four shrugged off winter flooding, with few if any subsequent ill effects. The seasonal differences were expected, since previous research has shown that dormant plants are much better at tolerating flooding than those in active growth. But the more or less complete indifference to winter flooding was unexpected. Indeed these Mediterranean plants turned out to be less bothered by flooding than many plants of more-moist soils, such as wheat and soybean.

The exact reasons for their flooding tolerance are unknown, but an intriguing possibility is that their tolerance of drought may be part of the answer. Waterlogging, and the accompanying lack of oxygen, can stop roots working properly, meaning that a flooded plant can experience 'physiological drought', even though there's no actual shortage of water. Plants that routinely deal with *real* drought may be well equipped to deal with this.

What does this mean for gardeners? The researchers caution against getting carried away, but it looks like the likelihood of flooding shouldn't automatically rule out these, and possibly other, Mediterranean plants. I would only add that the pot experiments used decent potting compost, while Wisley's soil is a sandy loam; I can't help wondering what would happen on a heavy clay soil.

Full marks, by the way, to the Royal Horticultural Society for funding this work.

Plants to keep you cool, and quiet

Every year around this time, the RHS hosts its annual John MacLeod Lecture. The lecture, named after a former professor of horticulture at the RHS, was created to highlight important and inspiring topics in horticultural science. This year's lecture, on 10 November, will be given by Dr Ross Cameron from the University of Sheffield. The lecture is entitled 'Urban Horticulture – Repairing the Rift?', and in it Ross will describe the many benefits horticulture (and plants in general) provide to those of us who live in towns and cities.

This is a big subject, much of it needing no introduction to keen gardeners; for example, we don't need telling that gardening keeps you fit and makes you feel better (at least most of the time). However, I want here to focus on something slightly different. Specifically (to get the jargon out of the way at the start), the way in which 'green infrastructure' (i.e. plants) provides 'ecosystem services' such as regulation of air temperature, noise and pollution, reduction of run-off and flooding, and thermal insulation for buildings.

Of course we've known for some time that plants do all these useful things. But the obvious fact that *any* plant

189

is vastly superior to tarmac, concrete or bare soil has rather blinded us to the fact that some plants do them so much better than others. Recent research in this area is reported in a paper in the journal *Annals of Botany* by Ross and his co-author Tijana Blanuša.

More frequent heatwaves are just one of the unpleasant consequences of climate change and, even in Britain, cities can become dangerously hot in summer. Although plants can help a lot, it helps to understand that they do so in at least three different ways: by shading, by evaporative cooling, and by reflecting sunlight. It's tough to find plants that do all three well, but research shows that in the UK evaporative cooling may be most important, and is maximised by fast-growing trees with spreading, multi-layered canopies.

At the opposite temperature extreme, buildings sheltered by trees and shrubs lose less heat in the winter. One recent study compared cherry laurel and *Cotoneaster franchetii*. The former provided better insulation, but overall the latter was a better choice – at least for a sunny wall – since its smaller leaves and less dense canopy still provided some insulation, but also allowed more sunlight to penetrate during the day.

Another climatic hazard, much in the news recently, is flooding. All trees massively reduce the amount and velocity of water reaching the ground but, as usual, some are better than others. A large canopy with extensive branching helps, but so does the 'fine-textured' canopy of many evergreen conifers. Even bark texture turns out to be important; the rough, grooved bark of red oak retains two-and-a-half times more water than the smooth bark of *Betula lenta*.

Trees and shrubs also intercept dust, pollution and noise – important if you live near a busy road. One Italian study found that lime and plane were better at capturing the smallest (and most dangerous) particles from diesel engines, while oaks were better at capturing larger particles. A UK study found that Corsican pine was very effective at capturing particles of all sizes.

Dense plantings of shrubs, ideally a few metres taller than the receiver of the noise, are best for reducing noise. Species with dense foliage and low forking branches work best; one study found that bamboos fitted the bill perfectly. Studies also show that at least some of the effect of a noise-reducing shelter belt are psychological; noise doesn't seem so bad if you can't see where it's coming from.

It's still early days for figuring out which plants are best for improving the urban environment, and especially finding those really useful plants that can provide two or three different services. But the basic point is one I've made before: when it comes to saving the planet, don't make the mistake of overlooking the importance of gardening.

My New Zealand favourites

Plants from New Zealand are common enough in British gardens. Nearly all of us grow a hebe or two, and phormiums and pittosporums are popular too. But on a recent trip to New Zealand, I started to wonder if there were other New Zealand plants that ought to be more widely grown. In the end I came up with two that impressed me, both in gardens and in the wild.* Both are also unfamiliar members of familiar genera.

Cordyline australis, the New Zealand cabbage tree, is a frequent sight in warmer gardens, and has been adopted as a kind of unofficial emblem by Torquay, where it is known as the 'Torbay palm', even though it's unrelated to true palms. Much more interesting is the mountain cabbage tree, *C. indivisa*, a strikingly attractive plant that makes its common cousin look as dull as, well, cabbage. With its broad, blue-grey leaves atop a trunk up to 8m tall, it's a really spectacular, dramatic plant for the 'tropical' garden.

Mystery surrounds its hardiness. The ordinary cabbage tree is hardy only in warmer gardens, and the mountain cabbage tree is frequently said to be even less hardy, perhaps

---

* In my new garden in Devon, I'm trying to grow both. Roy Lancaster very kindly gave me the *Cordyline*, so if it dies, you may never hear from me again.

only a conservatory plant. Yet, as its name suggests, it grows at higher altitudes than the common species, where winters can be really quite unpleasant. December 2010 reduced some borderline plants to mush at Inverewe Garden in Scotland, but the mountain cabbage tree sailed through without a scratch. Maybe a reputation for tenderness comes from a tendency to die suddenly and unexpectedly, especially when young. But don't let that put you off; give it plenty of water, a humus-rich soil, some shelter and a bit of light shade, and you should be OK. And if you are, trust me, you won't regret it.

My second choice is a fuchsia. And before you tell me you grow fuchsias already, let me assure you this is a fuchsia like no other. There are at least 100 species of fuchsia, all but four of them from South and Central America, and it's from these American species that all our modern showy hybrids are derived. New Zealand has three species, and *F. excorticata* is the biggest in the whole genus. We're used to thinking of fuchsias as shrubs, but *F. excorticata* is a proper small tree, up to 12m in the wild. So tall in fact that you sometimes don't notice it's there, until you look down and realise you're walking on a carpet of fallen red flowers.

Its flowers, which are produced all along the branches in spring, are hard to describe. Green buds open to a metallic purple, before eventually turning deep red. Later there are sweet, aromatic berries, much prized by the Māoris and made into jam by early European settlers. As a young shrub the plant itself is nothing remarkable, but be patient; the trunk and branches of mature trees have beautiful golden, peeling bark and eventually become quite shaggy. If you like *Acer griseum*, you will love *F. excorticata*.

The New Zealand tree fuchsia is hardy in milder gardens, but worth trying in a sheltered spot almost anywhere. It's fast-growing too, so even worth a go from seed. If your gardening friends are excited by our modern, overblown hybrid fuchsias, don't expect them to even notice this one, but more discerning visitors will be impressed.

Hemiparasites for gardeners

Growing one or two parasitic plants is practically mainstream gardening these days. Some of us have probably tried to establish mistletoe on an old apple tree, and one or two may even have succeeded. And anyone with serious pretensions of achieving a functioning wildflower meadow will have tried sowing *Rhinanthus minor* (yellow rattle) by now. If getting yellow rattle established is proving difficult, there are a couple of things you need to remember. One is that its seeds require winter chilling to break dormancy, so it's essential that seeds are sown in summer or autumn, prefer-ably as soon as they're ripe. Another is that yellow rattle is an annual, and that its seeds do not persist in the soil, so it's very easy to wipe out a healthy population by cutting the vegetation before it's had chance to seed. Cutting *must* be left until its seeds have ripened.

Both mistletoe and yellow rattle are technically *hemipa-rasites*. That is, both have chlorophyll and photosynthesise normally, but they steal water and nutrients from their host plant. Yellow rattle's fondness for attaching itself to the roots of vigorous grasses, and consequently reducing their vigour, is why it's such a useful plant in a wildflower meadow. But my own experience suggests that you can't expect yellow rattle to establish in the face of really vigorous grass on a rich soil – you must have run down the fertility a bit to give it a fighting chance. In fact I'd almost say yellow rattle is quite a good way to test if you have any real hope of establishing an interesting meadow; sprinkle on some seeds, and if you never see them again, your soil is probably still too fertile.

So is that it, or are there other hemiparasites you might consider growing? Leafing through an old copy of the RHS magazine *The Plantsman* the other day, I came across an article on growing the American genus *Castilleja*, commonly known as Indian paintbrush. *Castilleja* is very beautiful, with the many species having showy flowers in every shade from red through orange to pink and yellow, so you certainly might want to try. Surprisingly, the *European Garden Flora*, the bible of everything grown by European gardeners, doesn't mention them at all.

The *Plantsman* article came to the conclusion that *Castilleja can* be grown on its own, but that such plants never grow as well as those attached to a host. One of the very few nurseries that even tries to grow hemiparasites is Kevock Garden Plants, near Edinburgh, so I took the opportunity of talking to someone on their exhibit (a well-deserved gold, by the way) in the Great Pavilion at Chelsea the other week. Apparently they struggle to grow *Castilleja*, and other hemiparasites, which is why there were none in their catalogue, or in their exhibit. But they would be happy to talk to anyone who was willing to investigate the best way of growing them, and what their preferred hosts are. One suggestion is that the much more familiar American native *Penstemon* might make a good host, and I can see *Penstemon* and *Castilleja* making a fetching combination. If you decide to grow *Castilleja*, with or without *Penstemon*, I can more or less guarantee you'll be the only gardener in the neighbourhood who does.

What about other native hemiparasites? *Euphrasia* (eyebright) is very pretty and a common sight in short grassland throughout the country, but is definitely a plant of pastures rather than meadows, so probably no use for even moderately tall vegetation. Bigger, in fact about the same size as yellow rattle, and so maybe worth a try in a meadow, is *Odontites vernus* (red bartsia). But neither eyebright nor red bartsia are in the *RHS Plant Finder* or the *European Garden Flora*, so if you fancy growing either, you're on your own. The *European Garden Flora* does suggest that a few species of another relative of yellow rattle, *Pedicularis* or lousewort, may have been grown in the past, but it's unlikely they have ever been in general cultivation (*Pedicularis* is another plant that Kevock have trouble with). Britain has two native louseworts, both attractive but rather small plants, relatively common in heaths and bogs, but I never heard of anyone trying to grow either in a garden.

That leaves *Parentucellia* (yellow bartsia), for my money our most attractive native hemiparasite, not that uncommon near the coast in Devon and Cornwall. *The Plant Finder* doesn't list any suppliers, but the UK Biological Records Centre says it 'has increased northwards and eastwards in Britain, largely through introductions from seed mixtures'. Which suggests it must be in cultivation, since it doesn't seem common enough to be an accidental contaminant. It also seems to be quite a common weed of waste ground in New Zealand, so it can't be hard to grow. Finding the seeds may be a problem, but I noticed some for sale on eBay. Definitely worth a try if you can find the seeds; let me know how you get on.

Total parasites for gardeners

Many gardeners are familiar with hemiparasites, at least in the form of yellow rattle. But complete parasites – plants that lack chlorophyll and steal all their needs from a host – are almost unknown to gardeners, and you can see why when you look at some of them. Dodder (*Cuscuta*) is related to bindweed, but is even less attractive. A dodder seedling starts off in the ground, but once it twines round and attaches itself to a host, the root dies and it sucks everything it needs from its victim's stem. Both our species are quite rare, but the commoner of the two mainly attacks heather and gorse, and a thoroughly infested gorse bush can look like it's completely submerged by a carpet of red string. Unsurprisingly, *Cuscuta* appears not be in cultivation.

Another group of complete parasites are the broom-rapes. We have quite a few species, but they're all quite rare and rather inconspicuous, so you're unlikely to notice them at all unless you set out to find them. One or two species can be grown in gardens if you try hard, but since they lack both leaves and chlorophyll and are basically brown, I wouldn't bother unless your main aim in life is to grow something that none of your neighbours has even considered growing.

Again, *The Plant Finder* doesn't list any suppliers. In Spain, one broomrape (*Orobanche crenata*) is quite a bad weed, attaching itself to beans, peas or sunflowers. Also in Spain is *Cytinus hypocistis*, a curious plant that lives entirely inside the roots of *Cistus* and *Halimium* – the only part that ever appears above ground is the striking yellow or red flowers that appear at ground level in spring. These are really quite attractive, but I've no idea whether anyone has even tried to grow *Cytinus* in a garden. You can't buy it, so your only hope is to take a walk in the hills of Andalusia in summer and collect some berries, each of which contains thousands of extremely tiny seeds. Sprinkle these around a *Cistus* bush and see what happens – but don't hold your breath, and please don't blame me if nothing happens.

One complete parasite that definitely is in cultivation is *Lathraea clandestina* (purple toothwort), bursting out of the ground in spring like an extra from *The Evil Dead*. Purple toothwort is one of those plants that seems to have narrowly escaped being a British native, growing wild just across the Channel in Belgium and France. But toothwort has also escaped into the wild in a few places in Britain; like *Cytinus*, it lives completely underground, appearing above ground only at flowering time. The reference books say it's parasitic on the roots of willows and poplars, and the plant in the Botanical Gardens here in Sheffield grows on a large black poplar. Most other records are also on willows and poplars, but there are also records on hawthorn, birch, beech, hazel and various conifers. At RHS Wisley, with a vast array of victims to choose from, it's so far been found on silver maple, rhododendrons, *Erica*, *Calluna*, *Metasequoia*, holly and hazel.

Other recorded hosts include box, hornbeam, bamboo (species unknown), walnut, *Gunnera* and *Cercidiphyllum* (katsura). In Ireland it's been found on *Cordyline australis* (cabbage tree), *Nyssa sylvatica* (tupelo), Lawson's cypress and even *Kniphofia* (red-hot poker). Some of the weirdest records come from its native France: vines, dogwood, spindle, brambles, *Arum* (lords and ladies), *Ornithogalum* (star of Bethlehem) and – bizarrely – *Crithmum maritimum* (rock samphire). How a plant that shows a distinct preference for shady spots by streams ever came to be found on a sea cliff (for samphire grows nowhere else) is a complete mystery, at least to me.

Apart from Wisley, other places to see it include Kew, Wakehurst Place, Hidcote, Cambridge Botanic Garden, and the Royal Botanic Garden, Edinburgh. Roy Lancaster is apparently a fan, and the colony at the Sir Harold Hillier Gardens in Hampshire was introduced by him from Cambridge. Roy has also noticed it growing on *Sophora japonica* (Japanese pagoda tree) and *Magnolia* × *veitchii* at Nymans Garden in West Sussex.

Purple toothwort really is quite attractive, if a little creepy. If you want to grow it, *The Plant Finder* lists only one current supplier. The quickest option may be to find some-one who already has a plant and can dig you up a section of parasitised root, but even then it may take three years for flowers to appear. The large round seeds are easy to collect as long as you get to them before they are perfectly ripe, at which point the plant fires them a surprisingly long way, like peas out of a pea-shooter. Starting with seed, however, is only for the very patient, since plants may take up to ten years to flower. Worth the wait though, for anyone with a really tough, shady patch where *nothing* else will grow. After all, it's not every day you come across a garden plant that will grow in total darkness.

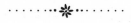

Cold comfort for seeds

Look online for advice on germinating seeds that need a period of winter chilling to break dormancy, and it won't be long before you come across the following, or something like it: 'sow your seeds in a pot and leave outside to let frost break down the seed coat.' Which is reasonable enough advice, and quite likely to work, but I'm a firm believer that you're a better gardener if you know not just what you're doing, but why you're doing it, and that isn't quite right.

If a seed needs cold, it's generally to do one of two things, and sometimes both. Some seeds have an immature embryo that will only grow to full size at low temperatures. Other seeds (the majority) simply have a chemical switch that is turned from 'off' to 'on' by a cold period. In neither case does this have much to do with the seed coat.

Nor does it have anything at all to do with frost. If a seed needs cold to break dormancy, the exact temperature required varies from species to species, but anything below 10°C is usually OK. Mentioning frost could lead you to believe that your seeds need to be frozen, which they don't; frozen seeds will just stay dormant. Something else that I've been guilty of assuming is obvious, but perhaps isn't, is that for the cold to work seeds need to be wet, or technically *imbibed*. Low temperatures will not break the dormancy of dry seeds.

Not surprisingly, seed dormancy broken by winter chilling is common among species that live in places with cold winters. Thus it's only natural to assume that it becomes more frequent as winters get colder, so I've also seen it suggested that it's particularly common among alpines. But it's not; in fact, outside tropical rain forest (which has the lowest proportion of species with seed dormancy), alpine floras have the smallest proportion of species with seed dormancy of any habitat. To understand why we need to think about what seed dormancy is actually doing.

Dormancy is a way to persuade the seed not to germinate at a time that might not be good for it, and instead to germinate at a time when the young plant is more likely to thrive. So it may have nothing to do with cold; in parts of the world where fires are frequent, for example, seeds often have dormancy that has evolved to ensure they germinate *after* a fire rather than *before* one.

But in climates with cold winters, seed dormancy is usually there to make sure seeds germinate in spring rather than in autumn, and two things make that less necessary in alpine habitats. First, alpine winters are so severe that a simple requirement for moderately high temperatures for germination is enough to prevent germination in autumn; by the time seeds are shed, it's already too cold for them to germinate. And second, remember that to break dormancy seeds need to be cold, but not frozen, so alpine winters are mostly too *cold* to break dormancy.

But whether or not you care about exactly what happens when you sow dormant seeds, the original advice is still pretty good: sow your seeds outdoors as soon as they are ripe, and then leave them alone for as long as it takes. Whatever they need to make them germinate, Mother Nature will supply it eventually.

Barriers for slugs and snails

It's always entertaining when *The Garden* and *Which? Gardening* drop onto the doormat on the same day, offering competing advice on the same topic. A while ago now the RHS magazine *The Garden* suggested 'greener' ways of dealing with slugs and snails. An important topic, since many of us are trying to garden more sustainably, and slugs and snails regularly top gardeners' 'most hated' list.

The Garden's view, quite reasonably, is that almost anything is greener than using metaldehyde pellets, whose safety for garden wildlife is somewhat suspect. Their advice on the alternatives is also pretty sensible. Nematodes are good, but they're expensive, the soil has to be warm enough, and they don't work on snails. And ferric phosphate slug pellets work just as well as metaldehyde, so there really is no excuse for any of us continuing to use metaldehyde.*

The Garden also suggests collecting slugs and snails by torchlight, which probably does reduce numbers, but I think requires a level of dedication that few of us possess; maybe pay the kids to do it, so much per head? Beer-filled traps must reduce numbers too, but do they do enough

---

* Metaldehyde looks likely to be banned soon, although at the time of writing the position is confused, owing to a legal challenge to the proposed ban.

unless deployed in unrealistic numbers? I'm not sure they do.

The Garden also recommends copper tape or collars, and barriers such as sharp sand or grit. Such barriers, as it happens, were the subject of a trial in the contemporaneous issue of *Which? Gardening*. I must admit I was amazed by the range of weird and wonderful barriers available – a testament, I suppose, to the fear induced in gardeners by molluscs. Copper tape, copper-impregnated 'Shocka' mat, a plastic barricade akin to a medieval fortification, granules from Doff and Westland, and even plain old sandpaper (cheap at least) were all trialled and found wanting. None had the slightest effect, and in fact sandpaper and the Westland granules made slug damage worse than using nothing at all.

The failure of copper tape is interesting, because copper has proved highly effective at deterring slugs under lab conditions, which I guess shows the dangers in extrapolating from such conditions to the much more realistic conditions used by *Which?*. Other slug deterrents that have proved effective in the lab, and which I offer here with no guarantee or recommendation at all, include garlic and hemlock. But take care with hemlock, which is just as likely to poison you as it is your slugs.

Returning to the *Which?* trial, a different kind of barrier, in the form of a ready-made liquid from Grazers that you spray on your crops, didn't work either; in fact sprayed plants suffered more damage than unsprayed ones. Grazers' original spray, designed to repel rabbits, pigeons and deer, has been around for a while, and when *Which?* tested that, it seemed to work at least some of the time. Both versions share the same active ingredient: calcium chloride. I can't find any published information on the effect of calcium chloride on molluscs, but one study found that garden snails strongly prefer to eat plants that are rich in calcium. So my guess would be that calcium chloride just makes plants a bit tastier, which would certainly be consistent with the *Which?* trial results.

Simple Sowing Natural Slug and Snail Barrier represents a completely different approach to the problem. A tape containing seeds makes a protective barrier of antirrhinum, cynoglossum, dianthus, dracocephalum, nigella, penstemon, rudbeckia and zinnia around your crops. Pretty too, which is just as well since it had no effect on slugs or snails in the *Which?* trials.

Better – but still not wonderful – were Vitax Slug Gone Wool Pellets. This hairy barrier really did seem to repel slugs, at least at first, although the effect wore off during the trial. But there was some suggestion that it might have reduced growth of the test plants. Finally, and best of all (but still far from a Best Buy) was Doff Slug Defence Gel. This repelled slugs and snails, but tended to be washed away after a few days, so you would have to keep applying it. Sadly, we don't know what's in it, apart from 'natural ingredients'; exactly which natural ingredients is a commercial secret.

And that's the lot – not a real winner among them. Along with earlier trials of homemade barriers, such as egg shells, soot or coffee grounds, which also don't work, it looks like slug and snail barrier technology is still waiting for its breakthrough moment.

. . . . **❋** . . . .

DIY slug gel

Readers may recall my report on a *Which? Gardening* trial of slug and snail barriers. Most were completely useless, a result recently confirmed by research at the RHS. Best of the bunch was Doff Slug Defence Gel, which certainly works, but tended to be washed away after a few days, which was enough to prevent it being given the 'Best Buy' accolade.

As I noted at the time, a frustrating feature of Doff's gel is that we don't know what's in it, apart from 'natural ingredients'. Nothing for it but to ask Doff, which led to the following slightly *Alice in Wonderland* exchange:

Me: Can you possibly tell me what is in Doff organic
   slug defence gel, i.e. what is the active ingredient?

Doff: The product does not have an active ingredient, it
   is just a gel made from natural ingredients.

Me: OK. Can you tell me what those natural ingredients
   are? Or is it a secret?

Doff: I am not able to give out formulation details.

So a dead end there then. But recently a gardener from
The Netherlands got in touch to say that he had bought a
similar Dutch slug gel. He also found that it worked, but
like me it bothered him that he didn't know what was in
it. So he did some digging around and found an American
slug gel, sold by Wilco Distributors of California, which
does list its ingredients.

Apart from water, these are: sodium carboxymethyl
cellulose (aka CMC), potassium sorbate and 5% sodium
chloride. CMC is a thickener used in everything from ice
cream to cosmetics and paint, so that's what makes the gel.
Potassium sorbate is just a preservative, so the active ingredient is that good old slug nemesis common salt, which
certainly qualifies as a natural ingredient (although I'm not
so sure about CMC).

Now you know that, there's nothing to stop you making your own. You can buy CMC from Amazon at £16 a
kilo. Making the gel takes about 40g of CMC per litre of

water, add 5% salt and you have your own slug gel. You don't need the potassium sorbate, which is only necessary for a commercial product that has to have a long shelf life. Since a kilo of CMC makes about 25 litres of gel, and 50g of salt costs almost nothing, that's a lot less than £1 per litre, compared to about £6 for a litre of Doff.

For the adventurous among you, there may be other options for the gel itself. Anyone who has ever tried hanging wallpaper will inevitably have half a packet of old wallpaper paste somewhere in the shed, so you could always try that. It may not be very persistent, but according to *Which?* neither was the Doff version.

One thing to bear in mind with any salt-based slug barrier is that if you consistently use a lot in one place, it will eventually make your soil salty, and most plants won't like that. But as long as you don't overdo it, the salt should be washed out by the rain before it becomes a problem.

Prepare for the end of chemical warfare

Remember sodium chlorate? Before 1940 that was about the only chemical option for killing weeds. But it is a very powerful oxidising agent, and therefore left dead vegetation, or indeed any organic matter, liable to burst into flames. In the 1930s, New Zealand farmers famously suffered an epidemic of 'exploding trousers', owing to the widespread use of sodium chlorate to control ragwort.

From the 1940s to the 1960s organic chemists were falling over themselves to devise new chemicals for killing weeds. Older gardeners will recall 2,4,5-T, simazine, atrazine, diuron, paraquat and others as practically ubiquitous. But today the golden age of weedkillers is over. It gradually became apparent that these chemicals were very nasty indeed and approval for their use, including all those listed above, has gradually been withdrawn. Even good old sodium chlorate finally met its Waterloo in 2009.

Which leaves glyphosate, a deceptively simple molecule first reported in 1971. Its approval for use in the EU was due to expire on 15 December 2017, and its eventual reapproval has been one long cliff-hanger that has gone right up to the wire. The European Commission first drafted a new regulation for reapproval in mid-June 2016. A minor concession to concerns about glyphosate's safety was that the regulation proposed renewal for ten years, rather than the usual fifteen years. But votes at successive meetings of the relevant committee failed to achieve a qualified majority (don't ask) and glyphosate remained in limbo. Finally a redrafted regulation that proposed renewal for just five years was enough to persuade Germany to change sides, thus achieving the necessary qualified majority. France and Italy remain opposed, while the UK has supported reapproval throughout.

This is an early Christmas present for Monsanto, and for all those who like to have a chemical solution to their weed problems. But it's a result that was achieved only by a concerted effort to rubbish the original World Health Organisation (WHO) report, which declared in March 2015 that glyphosate was 'probably carcinogenic'. I don't think I can do better than quote one of several comments by WHO's cancer research agency (IARC) on the subject:

> Following the classification of glyphosate in March 2015 as *probably carcinogenic to humans* (Group 2A) by the IARC Monographs Programme, IARC has been the target of an unprecedented number of orchestrated actions by stakeholders seeking to undermine its credibility – reminiscent of strategies used by the tobacco industry several decades ago. Experts who participated in the evaluation have been directly targeted with false statements, received letters from industry lawyers requesting provision of Monographs draft documents and related materials, and some have been deposed and subpoenaed in relation to ongoing legal cases which the industry is defending in the United States.
>
> In the interest of transparency, IARC has documented

some of these instances, and our responses can be found on the Agency's website.

The latest attempts to discredit the IARC classification have involved contacting experts taking part in the glyphosate evaluation, asking them to comment on preliminary drafts of the Monographs, perhaps in order to identify potential disagreements or inconsistencies between the Working Group members.

Deliberative drafts are confidential precisely in order to protect the Working Group from interference by vested interests.

I think we can safely say that getting glyphosate past the regulators will be even more difficult in five years' time, and it's only a matter of time before it goes the way of DDT and smoking in pubs. Thoughtful gardeners should start planning to garden without it after 2022.

Tea bags

A tea bag doesn't look like much, does it? And a used tea bag, tossed casually in the bin, hardly seems worth a moment's thought. Yet in Britain we drink 165 million cups of tea every day, and 96% of those are made with a bag, so that's a little over 158 million tea bags per day. Even if you can't picture a great steaming heap of 158 million used tea bags (no, neither can I), that clearly is worth a thought.

In fact, several thoughts. The first is that over 57 billion tea bags per year is quite a lot of landfill. Most of us have gardens, and if you have a garden but don't have a compost heap, in my opinion you have some explaining to do. If you do have a compost heap, as you should, then that is your tea bag's natural destination. Tea bags are just another variety of green waste, along with garden waste, kitchen vegetable waste, and almost anything else that used to be alive, including coffee grounds, hair, egg boxes, cereal packets, vacuum-cleaner dust (mainly dust mites and flakes of human skin, and therefore highly nutritious), nail clippings, rabbit or hamster bedding, general floor sweepings and old cotton or wool clothing.

Tea bags are, after all, just leaves. Mostly tea, of course, *Camellia sinensis*. Tea leaves will break down in your compost heap, just like all the other leaves (e.g. lawn clippings, weeds etc.) that normally go in there. In fact, ecologists who are interested in how the environment affects decomposition have proposed using tea bags as a standard reference that can be bought and used anywhere in the world. However, they want a tea bag that will stay in one piece when buried, so they can measure decomposition of its contents. There is such a tea bag, in which the bag is plastic, but that's very unusual; not only that, it's emphatically *not* what you want in your compost heap.

Fortunately, in the overwhelming majority of British tea bags, the bag itself is made, rather surprisingly, from bananas. Not the ubiquitous yellow fruit, but the closely related *Musa textilis*: abacá or Manila hemp. The fibre from the leaf stalks of abacá is both strong and fine, in fact just what you want for tea bags and other specialised paper products such as filter paper and banknotes. But despite its strength, once in your compost heap the bag will break down just like any other vegetable matter.

You will occasionally read that tea bags are not entirely biodegradable, which is true – up to a point. So that the bag will seal properly, it contains a very small quantity of the plastic polypropylene, which melts when heated and so can be used to make a secure seal. But although polypropylene does not break down in the compost heap, it does break up, so it's hard to find any trace of a tea bag after six months in a compost heap. Moreover the quantity involved is minute, scarcely a drop in the ocean compared to other plastic waste, such as carrier bags, bottles and plastic packaging.*

---

* In the wake of the publicity about single-use plastic, more and more manufacturers are now making plastic-free tea bags. Alternatively you could drink loose leaf tea, which also tastes better.

But never mind what you can do for tea bags, what can tea bags do for you? Few gardeners can make enough of their own compost, so it pays not to ignore any source of organic matter. There may be only just over 3g of tea in a single tea bag, but that's still over 180,000kg of useful organic matter every year (dry weight – obviously a lot more in the soggy state). Nor should we ignore the bag itself, which is about one tenth of the weight of the tea.

In addition, although it's the bulky organic content of compost that improves soil structure, retains moisture and suppresses weeds, there are useful plant nutrients in there too, and here again tea bags can make a contribution. As leaves go, tea is actually towards the high end of nutrient concentrations, with about 4% nitrogen and about 0.5% phosphorus, so Britain's annual consumption of tea bags represents over 7,000kg of nitrogen and nearly 1,000kg of phosphorus. All things considered, one thing's for sure – used tea bags are far too valuable to just throw away.

This article originally appeared on the website of the UK Tea & Infusions Association (tea.co.uk).

The last word on tree planting

At West Dean, a book about one of my favourite gardens, by two of my favourite gardeners, is so crammed with good advice that I had to ration myself to a few pages at a time, to make sure I was taking it all in. For example, you may never be required to manufacture your own steel lawn edging, but once you've read Jim Buckland's description of how it's done, you would never consider doing it any other way.

But even in such exalted company, Jim's page on How To Plant A Tree is so good that it stands out. Here it is, in a nutshell:

- Plant the best and smallest tree you can find, ideally a bare-root maiden (one-year-old). Compared to a larger tree, it will be cheaper, establish better, and it won't need staking.

- Put nothing other than soil in the planting hole.

- Use fertiliser only in the most impoverished soil, and never in the first year.

- Keep a minimum of 1m in all directions free of other vegetation. Mulch this area well, but at least 5cm away from the trunk.

🖎 Plant when the tree is dormant, and water thoroughly every seven to ten days in the first season if the weather is dry.

🖎 If formative pruning is required, start right away, but don't overdo it.

And last but not least: put the right tree in the right place. Despite this being the most important advice of all (Jim actually puts it first, where it belongs), it's probably the hardest to get right. Unless you're a tree expert, how do you choose the right tree?

Which brings me neatly to another source of good advice: the Trees and Design Action Group (TDAG; http://www.tdag.org.uk/). TDAG is a charity whose mission is to 'increase awareness of the role of trees in the built environment'. There's a lot more to that than just choosing the right tree, but one of its published guides does just that. It's aimed primarily at people who plant trees for a living, but that doesn't mean you can't use it too. At its core is the Tree Selector, which takes you through a list of criteria to find the right tree for you. You can do this the hard way, via the written guide, or download a spreadsheet that you can rapidly sort to produce a shortlist of candidates.

For example, if you want a tree for a small garden but also suitable for a coastal site, you very quickly find yourself with just 28 candidates, mainly species of tamarisk, hawthorn, holly and pear, plus a few other things. You can then read about all of them in the detailed profiles and decide which one you like. Or, if that's too many, you can add another criterion, such as evergreen foliage, which leaves just seven candidates, or a weeping habit, which scores a bullseye – *Pyrus salicifolia*.

TDAG also has information that, at least as far as I know, isn't all that easy to find anywhere else. For example, suppose you'd like a magnolia, but for a slightly dodgy site that might be a bit waterlogged. Is there a magnolia for you? Yes there is, but only one: *Magnolia stellata*. And in case you were hoping *M. stellata* had passed on this trait to its popular hybrid, *M. × loebneri*, I'm sorry to tell you it hasn't.

In short, use TDAG to choose a tree and Jim's advice on how to plant it, and success is as close to guaranteed as anything can be in this world.

Viburnum leaf beetle

Time was when viburnums were relatively pest-free. But that was before the arrival from Europe of the dreaded viburnum beetle, now one of Britain's top pests of ornamental plants. There's some damage by the adults in summer, but the chief problem is the larvae in spring, which can leave susceptible species looking like a lace doily.

The first thing to consider, if you're planning on growing shrubs in a genus like *Viburnum*, where there is plenty of choice, is to think about growing the less susceptible species or cultivars. *Viburnum opulus* and *V. tinus*, for example, can both be completely shredded by the beetle, but several of the more attractive species are reasonably resistant. Cornell University have a good web page on susceptibility of the different species, and although it is based on observations in North America, it's probably generally applicable here too: http://www.hort.cornell.edu/vlb/suscept.html.

The good news is that some of the best Asian species are quite resistant, e.g. *V. carlesii*, *V. plicatum* and the hybrids *V.* × *burkwoodii* and *V.* × *bodnantense*. Best of all, my very favourite viburnum, *V.* × *juddii* (compact, beautiful and intensely fragrant), is highly resistant.

But as well as growing resistant species, it also helps to know your enemy. Work in North America, where they have even more trouble with viburnum leaf beetle than we do, reveals a complex relationship between the beetle and its host.

Female beetles chew through the bark of viburnum twigs and excavate cavities in the underlying pith. There they lay eggs in groups of about eight, covering them with frass (poo). Eggs overwinter in these cavities, protected from desiccation and predators. What's more, where the beetles choose to lay their eggs is by far the best guide to which species suffer the most damage; less susceptible species suffer less damage because the adults lay fewer eggs on them in the first place.

But viburnums are not defenceless in the face of this egg-laying behaviour. In response to the damage caused by the egg-laying females, infested twigs can mount a wound response, growing a callus tissue that either expels the eggs from the twig, or crushes the eggs and kills them. Naturally, the beetles don't take this lying down, and have their own counter-defence; namely, a strong preference for dead twigs for egg laying. Your initial reaction may be that that doesn't make much sense: what do the young larvae eat if they emerge onto a dead twig? But young larvae are highly mobile, and if there are live twigs not too far away, they soon find them and start munching.

As I'm sure you've already realised, this can quickly lead to a vicious circle, in which heavily-attacked shrubs have more dead twigs, which encourages more egg laying, which in turn leads to even more dieback, and so on. This can lead, in as little as two or three years, to the death of susceptible species like *V. opulus*.

But every cloud has a silver lining, and this behaviour also offers an opportunity for the gardener to intervene. Eggs are laid in the summer and remain dormant until the following spring, giving plenty of time to prune out any dead twigs, along with any eggs they may contain. If this is done in the early stages, when shrubs are still healthy and dieback is scarce, the chances are that a serious attack may never get going.

Is your lettuce what you think it is?

Plenty of people like to grow heritage vegetable varieties. Often they seem to taste better, although I wonder if that hasn't more to do with them being fresh, rather than having spent a week in a cold store followed by a few days on a supermarket shelf. But quite apart from their intrinsic qualities, growing something your great-grandparents might have grown provides an important connection with the past.

But there's a catch. You're never quite sure where an old variety has been, or how close it came to extinction before being rescued from the back of someone's shed. Which in turn means you can't be entirely sure that it's what it claims to be. A question that prompted three Dutch scientists, in research reported in the journal *Crop Science*, to check up on the lettuce seeds in the freezer at the Centre for Genetic Resources (CGN) at Wageningen University in The Netherlands. The closest analogue to the CGN in the UK would probably be somewhere like the National Institute of Agricultural Botany in Cambridge.

The CGN has a lot of different lettuce seeds (technically accessions), in fact 1,551 in all, 1,173 of which actually have a cultivar name attached. The question of whether such names are correct in some absolute sense is essentially unanswerable, so they asked the next best question: if two or more accessions have the same name, are they actually identical? 'The same name' means either exactly that, or a name known or commonly assumed to be a synonym. And 'identical' means at least 97.5% genetic similarity, based on 167 distinct genetic markers; in other words, no more than four of those markers were different. This value was chosen because plants undergo mutations all the time, so it's unreasonable to expect even samples of the same cultivar to be 100% identical.

The first thing to note in passing is that they took two samples from each accession, and in 5% of cases *they* weren't the same, so in some accessions not all the seeds in the same packet are identical.

But in the other 95%, how do you decide if a particular accession is what it claims to be? A good question, but not one with an easy answer. The researchers adopted the pragmatic approach of assuming that within a group of accessions with the same name, if two or more were identical, they were the real, authentic cultivar (on the grounds that two accessions are unlikely to be identical by chance). On that criterion, three-quarters of the CGN's lettuce accessions were authentic, and one quarter were not. In a surprising number of cases, *all* accessions with the same name were genetically different, leaving open the question of which (if any) is the 'true' cultivar. Things get worse as the cultivars become older; for cultivars released before 1900, only just over half were authentic.

The researchers then looked more closely at the two largest groups of supposedly identical cultivars, 'Sans Rivale à Graine Blanche' and 'Maikönig'. If neither of those names rings any bells, that's because the same plant is often sold under different names in different countries, and old varieties acquire names the ways ships acquire barnacles. Two common synonyms of 'Sans Rivale à Graine Blanche' are 'Attraction' and 'Bohemia'. Several accessions of 'Attraction' were 100% identical to each other and presumably authentic, but some were not. But not only did the CGN's three accessions of 'Bohemia' not belong to the main 'authentic' group, they were also very different from each other. From the genetic evidence, two of them appear to be completely different cultivars, and must presumably have simply become mislabelled at some time in their history.

At least synonyms of 'Maikönig' are just literal translations, i.e. 'Reina de Mayo', 'May Queen' etc., but that doesn't mean they're any more likely to be all the same thing. In particular, CGN's accession of 'May Queen', which is the name used in Britain, was genetically quite unlike 'Maikönig'. So don't even try to imagine what you might get if you buy 'May Queen' from a Dutch supplier; you'll just get a headache.

Worryingly, the CGN's lettuce seeds are probably a best-case scenario; they come from a recognised scientific genebank, and lettuce is largely self-pollinated, so at least it doesn't routinely acquire stray genes from whatever else happens to be growing in the neighbourhood. The bottom line for gardeners is that if a friend recommends a heritage cultivar, especially a pre-1900 one, the only way to be absolutely sure of growing the same plant is to scrounge some of their seeds; the chances of seeds with the same name from another supplier being the same are probably no better than evens. As for which (if either) is the right one, that's anybody's guess.

Wisdom from Which? Gardening

I'm a big fan of *Which? Gardening* (*W?G*). It's useful for all the things you would expect, such as finding the tastiest broad beans, the most comfortable secateurs, or the quietest shredder. But what I really like about *W?G* is their habit of asking questions that you either thought you already knew the answer to, or that had never occurred to you at all. Here are three nuggets from 2015 that illustrate both categories.

1. **Compost**. You may make your own garden compost, and I very much hope you do. But these days most local authorities have green-waste recycling that will do the job for you. So here's the question: are the results any different? You might expect them to be, since typical home-made compost is made rather slowly, at a low temperature, while green waste is composted much faster, at a high temperature.

W?G sent off some compost they had made themselves and some compost from a recycling centre to a lab to be analysed. There was only one sample of each, so you have to be a bit cautious about the result, but the differences were so large that they're probably generally true. The home-made compost had three times more nitrogen and five times more phosphorus than green-waste compost. Since other tests suggested the composts were about equally mature, the difference is almost certainly down to the raw material, with the green waste containing more woody material, which is much lower in nutrients.

Does that mean home-made compost is better? Not necessarily. The organic matter in compost, and its effect on soil structure, is more important than nutrients. Surveys also show that typical garden soil is high in nutrients already, and for some purposes, such as making your own potting compost for seed sowing, you might prefer low-nutrient compost. And bear in mind that if you compost your own softer waste, your garden is already a relatively closed system, with most of its nutrients being internally recycled, so any nutrients in 'imported' green-waste compost are just a bonus anyway.

2. **Tap water vs. rainwater**. Please sir, I know this one – tap water is better for acid lovers, especially in areas with hard water. *W?G* grew pelargoniums and gardenias in a Best Buy peat-based compost and watered them with either rainwater or tap water. Gardenias are well known to prefer an acid soil. The test was carried out in a hard water area, and tests showed that the rainwater was more acidic than pure water, while the tap water was more alkaline.

So what happened? Not a lot, but the plants watered with tap water were marginally better – even the gardenias. Analysis of the compost at the end of the four-month trial showed why; compost watered with rainwater was down to pH 4.5, which is too acid even for gardenias, although rhododendrons should still be OK. So, not exactly what you might have expected, although it would be nice to know what would have happened in a peat-free compost.

3. **Planting time**. *W?G* planted ten different perennials in autumn 2013 and spring 2014, at two very different sites, in Dorset and near Glasgow. One or two did best in autumn, or in spring, regardless of site, and penstemons didn't care, but six species did best when planted in autumn in Dorset and spring in Scotland. All the oriental poppies planted in autumn in Scotland died.

So at last, a trial where the answer you might have expected turned out, most of the time, to be the right one: in a cold climate, plant in spring; in a warm one, plant in autumn. But as *W?G* also point out, a lot also depends on your soil type and the vagaries of the weather. Not only that, autumn planting may not always be an option; *W?G* found that it was *much* easier to buy young, vigorous plants in spring.

ON BEING
A GARDENER

Green fingers are the test of a true Brit

I just tried answering a few practice UK citizenship tests. Just out of curiosity, since I'm allowed to be here already, but in any case they didn't seem all that difficult. My favourite question was 'John Constable (1776–1837) founded the modern police force in England. True or False?' But what slightly puzzled me was the complete absence of questions about something that I suspect is central to the character of many Brits: gardening. So I decided to have a go at rectifying the omission. Just a word of warning: in keeping with the spirit of the genuine test ('King Henry VIII's daughter Mary famously persecuted Protestants, and thus became known as Scary Mary. True or False?'), some of the wrong answers are not all that plausible.*

1. If your neighbour plants a leylandii 'hedge' and then neglects to prune it, once it reaches over 2m tall you are allowed to cut it down. True or False?

2. 80% of RHS members:
    a) Are women
    b) Live in Surrey
    c) Are under 30
    d) Live in caravans

* Answers on p. 269.

230

3. Which of the following was *not* a famous plant hunter?
   a) George Forrest
   b) Gabriel Oak
   c) David Douglas
   d) Reginald Farrer

4. Yellow rattle (*Rhinanthus minor*) is best grown in a:
   a) Pond
   b) Hanging basket
   c) Woodland garden
   d) Wildflower meadow

5. Which of the following gardens is *not* owned by the National Trust?
   a) Great Dixter
   b) Sissinghurst
   c) Hidcote
   d) Bodnant

6. The *Dahlia* genus is named after Roald Dahl. True or False?

7. The RHS's oldest garden is at Wisley in Surrey. Before it acquired Wisley, the Society's garden was in the London borough of:
   a) Chelsea

b) Chiswick

c) Lambeth

d) Richmond

8. Guernsey lily (*Nerine sarniensis*) comes originally from:

a) Jersey

b) Guernsey

c) South Africa

d) Madeira

9. Which of the following plants is a British native?

a) Snowdrop

b) Sweet chestnut

c) Sycamore

d) Foxglove

10. Living plants are mostly water, but their solid tissues are mostly made from:

a) Air

b) Water

c) Soil

d) Fertiliser

11. At the centenary Chelsea Flower Show in 2013, the RHS selected one of the best plants introduced during each of the previous ten decades, and invited gardeners

to vote for the 'Plant of the Centenary'. The winner was:

a)   *Geranium* Rozanne

b)   *Rosa* Peace

c)   *Erysimum* 'Bowles's Mauve'

d)   *Rhododendron yakushimanum*

If you get all those right, or even most of them, I reckon you deserve British citizenship, even if you don't know when the first Union Flag was created (1606, apparently), or when the Wars of the Roses started (search me).

Instagram-ready gardening

You know me, always keen to keep up with the latest trends. No, only joking, in fact you'd have to go a long way to find someone less aware of the latest fashion. Sometimes I never catch up with the latest cutting-edge technology, but even if I do, it's usually just as it's about to become obsolete and everyone else moves on to something new. And for all I know, *Zeitgeist* is a Swiss ski resort.

But I'm always keen to learn, so I was fascinated the other day to finally catch up with the Wyevale Garden

Centres Garden Trends Report 2018, in which Wyevale's experts combine their experience with surveys of gardeners to identify the latest gardening trends (yes, yes, I know the report was launched in March 2018, but see the first paragraph above). Much of the report seems to me like undiluted good news. More young gardeners are growing their own veg, and doing so organically, and the overwhelming majority of gardeners would like to attract more wildlife into their gardens. It's heartening to discover that 37% of British gardeners claim that wildlife is the most appealing feature of their gardens.

Some of the other trends seem reasonable enough, even if making sense of the detail isn't always easy. For example, smaller gardens mean more gardeners are exploiting vertical surfaces by growing climbers, so sales of climbers are up. But only one of their top ten best-selling climbers is a clematis, so it's hard to understand Wyevale's assertion that clematis account for over 60% of their climber sales. Nor is *C. montana*, the solitary clematis in the top ten, the obvious choice for anyone trying to garden in a small space. Other plants in the top ten are frustratingly non-specific; wisteria comes in at number 5, but wouldn't you love to know whether the Japanese or Chinese are ahead? You wouldn't? Well I would.

But it's when we get to the interface between gardening and social media that I start to feel my grip on reality loosening. Having only the vaguest notion of what Instagram is or does (see first paragraph again), I genuinely don't know what to make of the arrival of 'easy, pre-planted, Instagram-ready containers in subtler and greener colour ranges that keep up with the latest online trends'. As for the news that sales of cacti are up, 'partly down to their iconic looks suiting the social media age: they photograph brilliantly; the smaller specimens look great from above; and they are easy to incorporate into the Pinterest- and Instagram-friendly "flat-lay" technique', I feel that any comment from me would only make me look even more of a dinosaur than I am. Mind you, Wyevale also list their top five best-selling cacti, and since the top three are in plant families that are about as closely related to cacti as I am, I really don't know what to make of the whole cactus story.

Easier to understand are 'Social media's favourite flowers': apparently roses, peonies, zinnias, dahlias and hydrangeas. Here, finally, I think I begin to get the picture: plants with big, solid, round flowers or inflorescences, in other words, easy to photograph. Are we really entering an age when the plants we choose to grow depend on how easy they are to share on Facebook? I wonder what Gertrude Jekyll would have made of that?

Biodiversity for gardeners

Gardening, I hope we agree, is good for you, both mentally and physically. Gardens are also, as numerous studies have shown, full of wildlife. What has had researchers scratching their heads, though, is whether there's any connection between these two things. In other words, are people more relaxed, more comfortable, basically *happier*, in gardens with more wildlife? Or, to put that another way, is biodiversity good for you?

In one sense, the answer to that question is clear: when questioned, people generally express a strong preference for higher biodiversity. In one French study that questioned visitors to public gardens in Paris, more than 80% agreed that their feeling of well-being was improved by seeing lots of different flowers and birds. Even this result, however, has a sting in the tail. The overwhelming majority of biodiversity in gardens (and everywhere else) consists of insects and other invertebrates, but visitors were much more ambivalent about the value of insect diversity; only 37% felt their well-being was improved by a garden with lots of insects.

So much for valuing biodiversity in the abstract; it's when people encounter biodiversity in real life that things start to get really complicated. In a large study in Sheffield, visitors to numerous different riverside green spaces were questioned about their appreciation of biodiversity. The results were clear: participants were happier in places where they perceived a higher diversity of birds, butterflies, and plants. Unfortunately, these perceptions of biodiversity were at fault. When well-being was correlated with actual, measured biodiversity, it was increased only by bird diversity, showed no relationship with butterfly diversity, and actually declined with greater plant diversity.

The reasons for this apparent paradox are probably complex, but one contributory factor is surely that, in general, our natural-history skills are rubbish. The Sheffield researchers asked the participants to identify photographs of four birds, four plants and four butterflies, almost all of them common at the sites studied. Out of 1,108 people, two (0.002%) correctly identified all twelve pictures, while over a quarter couldn't name a single species. Given that the list included a blue tit, cow parsley and a peacock butterfly, it's clear how disconnected from nature many people are.

The French researchers found much the same. Asked to estimate the number of species of insects, flowers and birds in Paris gardens, the great majority of respondents gave drastic underestimates. Out of 1,116 garden visitors interviewed, nearly half guessed that the gardens contained only a single species of insect. Given the general invisibility of insects, maybe this isn't too surprising, but in direct contradiction to the evidence of their own eyes, 229 respondents thought the gardens contained only one flower species. The

French researchers also adopted an experimental approach, deliberately increasing biodiversity in some gardens, by providing nest boxes and planting pollinator-friendly plants, to see if anyone noticed. They didn't.

Nor is this confined to gardens. In a Swiss survey, 60% of respondents had never encountered the word 'biodiversity' at all. Asked to estimate the number of plant species in Switzerland, the median guess was 94,000, while the true figure is about 3,000. As the researchers who carried out the survey rather despondently noted, around 1,000 Swiss plant species are threatened to some extent, which doesn't seem like a hill of beans if you thought there were 94,000 to start with.

The lessons from all this are numerous, but here are just a couple. First, anything that helps to restore a connection with nature has got to be a good thing, and since most people's experience of nature takes place primarily in their own (or their parents') gardens, that must include getting more young people gardening. And second, professional biologists and conservationists should never make the mistake of thinking that the general public sees the world the same way they do.

The causes of hay fever

How's your botany today? Up to scratch? Or a bit below par? Maybe what you need is a bit of botanical accuracy.

I attended a conference last year where I had the pleasure of meeting Dr Lena Struwe, an American waging a one-woman war against botanical mistakes in commercial products, ingredients and images used in media, design, and advertising. A bit over the top, you might think, after all it's 'only' plants. But as Lena points out, how would you feel if someone served you horse meat, but said it was beef? After all, they're both herbivorous quadrupeds, quite similar from a distance, and scarcely distinguishable at all once they're in a lasagne.

One of Lena's recent campaigns, which you can read all about on her website (http://www.botanicalaccuracy.com/), is about the implied misinformation that comes with hay fever remedies. For some reason these are nearly always illustrated by pretty pictures of daisies, dandelions, thistles or fields of oil-seed rape. Anything, in fact, except the actual culprit, which is of course, at least 90% of the time, grass. For the simple reason that before pollen can give you hay fever, it has to get up your nose or into your eyes. And grass pollen, produced in vast quantities and readily blown around by the wind, is very likely to do that. Grass pollen is like this because grasses are pollinated by wind;

insect-pollinated plants (the great majority) produce much smaller quantities of sticky pollen, which is highly unlikely to get up your nose, unless you inhale a bee.

Unfortunately, the botanically-challenged people who design the adverts for hay fever remedies don't know this, or even if they do, they're determined not to let the facts get in the way of a pretty picture. So they promote the view, even if only subliminally, that dandelion pollen can give you hay fever (or even dandelion seeds, another inexplicably popular image).

But, I thought to myself as I read Lena's website, the stuff she's complaining about is American – surely *we* would never make that mistake? But of course, we do. The very first British website I checked had everything: field of oilseed rape, dandelion seeds, even some kind of legume in the act of being pollinated by a bee. One popular hay fever medicine comes in a box adorned with a sunflower, while a magazine feature on hay fever has a picture of a sneezing woman turning her head away from a bunch of roses.

The *Guardian* is wrong too, but in a more interesting way, with a feature on hay fever illustrated by a picture of a pine tree with the caption 'Beware trees … scots pine and silver birch'. Tree pollen can indeed be a cause of hay fever, especially early in the season, before grasses get going, but not pine. Yes, pine is wind pollinated, and yes, it produces vast quantities of pollen, but as the UN Food and

Agriculture Organisation notes: 'Some tree species produce large quantities of wind disseminated pollen that is not an important cause of hay fever. An outstanding example is the prodigious amount of pollen produced by species of pine, which has very little, if any, allergenic toxicity.'

Even the Boots website, which quite correctly says 'About 90% of people in the UK with hay fever are allergic to grass pollen', can't resist illustrating this statement with a picture that looks suspiciously like our old friend oil-seed rape. The problem, I assume, is the usual one that a little learning is a dangerous thing. We know enough to know that pollen comes from flowers, but many of us find it hard to believe that grass flowers really *are* flowers.

Still, it could be worse; juniper can give you hay fever, and it doesn't have flowers at all.

Science for gardeners

The Garden, the magazine of the Royal Horticultural Society, is 150 years old in 2016 and, slightly to my surprise, much of the celebratory content in the April 2016 birthday issue emphasised science. Sir Nicholas Bacon, RHS President, talked about how 'scientific advances and their wide-ranging consequences have been reflected and discussed in articles'. Alan Titchmarsh claimed *The Garden* 'crosses that great divide between academia and popularisation', while Ursula Buchan noted it was a window onto a 'rigorously scientific world'.

Now, I'm not averse to a bit of rigorous science when the occasion demands, but I think science can take a back seat most of the time. Of course, *The Garden* gives us the science when necessary; most recently, reporting the results of the RHS Plants for Bugs project, an experimental study of the effect of plant origin on garden wildlife. But articles in the birthday issue covered pruning evergreens, trials of flowering currants and annual sunflowers, the variety of beans available to UK gardeners, florists' tulips and profiles of a couple of gardens. Best of all, Roy Lancaster's selection of ten of the best woody garden plants introduced to British cultivation since 1866, which made me want to grow all those I don't grow already. All quite, and quite rightly, science-free.

Which set me thinking: why is science not relevant to gardeners more often? Clearly, the main reason is that gardening is often more of an art than a science. But even when we might expect science to be important, the nature of the subject matter sometimes gets in the way. As any ecologist will tell you, the world is a terribly variable place, and reasonably consistent rules are hard to come by. For example we know the great majority of plants are myc-orrhizal, and we know the partnership benefits plants, so why isn't the evidence for the benefit of adding mycorrhizas when planting much clearer than it is? I'm sure there are more reasons, but here are three: (1) We don't always add the right mycorrhiza; (2) mycorrhizas are very common, so most plants get infected by them whether we add them or not; and (3) much of what passes for 'gardening' might have been specifically designed to offend mycorrhizas.

At least we have a reasonable understanding of what mycorrhizas do. Sometimes the underlying science isn't clear at all; why should plants benefit from being sprayed with water that's had compost stirred into it, apart from the minor benefit of a few mineral nutrients? Given that every plant is different, every garden is different, and certainly every batch of compost tea is different, it's not surpris-ing that research on the effects of compost tea is highly inconsistent.

Maybe we sometimes expect a level of certainty that science simply isn't equipped to provide. Nests for solitary bees work really well in gardens, so why shouldn't nests for bumblebees work too? Nevertheless, exhaustive trials show that they don't. In the Sheffield BUGS project, we tried them in lots of gardens and not one was occupied. But I can't guarantee they will *never* work. Just as we know cigarettes kill most of the people who smoke them, but we all know someone (who knows someone) who smoked 40 a day and lived to be 100, artificial bumblebee nests are very occasionally used. And we are nothing if not a hopeful species, so why shouldn't our box be the lucky one? How else to account for the success of the Lottery?

Even when the evidence is crystal clear, we don't always believe it. Two large, careful studies show that rockdust does nothing. They even show *why*: it contains little of any use to plants, and the very little it does contain is released extremely slowly. The surprising thing about rockdust is not that it doesn't work, but that anyone ever thought it would. Yet rockdust remains on sale (as do bumblebee nest boxes), so people must still buy it.

Rigorous science is hard enough, but believing the results, especially in the face of commercial pressure to believe otherwise, can be even harder.

Gardening similes

There's nothing like a good simile for making your writing or speech more colourful. The arch-exponent of the art was Blackadder, where part of the fun was waiting for the next ridiculous example ('as happy as a Frenchman who's invented a pair of self-removing trousers' etc.). But you need to be careful if you decide to steal your material from an unfamiliar field.

What brought this to mind was reading columnist D.J. Taylor in the *Independent on Sunday*,* reflecting on TV coverage of the 2015 general election: 'Naturally, cliché abounded. Ukip's "2020 strategy" wound its way through the proceedings like knotweed through a lawn …'

The simile is a brilliant one, and captures perfectly the idea of two things inextricably knitted together. And knotweed certainly sounds the part, but is it? Several members of the genera *Fallopia* and *Persicaria* are known as knotweeds, but all are large plants, a metre or more tall, and none would last five minutes in a lawn. In any case, there are much better weeds that really do weave their way inseparably through lawns, such as white clover, slender speedwell and creeping buttercup.

Taylor has form in this area. A few years ago he was lamenting the rise of the sort of celebrity sports commentator who thinks he is more important than the event he is supposed to be describing: 'Over in radio-land the situation is in some respects even worse – not so much on account of the presence of ex-players adjusting to a new life-style, but

---

* Now sadly defunct, at least as a printed publication.

because the cult of personality winds through the proceedings like loosestrife through a hedge.'

Loosestrife? Like many common names, loosestrife is applied to two unrelated plants: purple loosestrife (*Lythrum salicaria* in the Lythraceae) and several yellow-flowered species of *Lysimachia* in the Primulaceae. But neither is commonly found winding through hedges, and again there are plenty of better alternatives: bindweed is the obvious choice, but also bryony, hop or goosegrass. If you have no idea what loosestrife is – and I suspect Taylor hasn't – perhaps it sounds like the sort of plant that ought to grow in hedges, but both sorts of loosestrife are herbaceous perennials, mostly of damp habitats.

If you're unfamiliar with purple loosestrife, the next time you're in Tate Britain, take a look at the nice clump towards the top right-hand corner of one of their most popular paintings: John Everett Millais' *Ophelia*. Does that look like a plant that winds through hedges? No it doesn't. Apparently Millais got it wrong anyway, since his loosestrife is supposed to be Shakespeare's 'long purples', which were actually early purple orchids. On the other hand, he got the right plant for the habitat, since you wouldn't expect early purple orchids on the river bank pictured in *Ophelia*.

How do we know Shakespeare meant the plants to be orchids (apart from believing what the Tate website says)? We know because the full quote from *Hamlet* is:

> There with fantastic garlands did she come
> Of crowflowers, nettles, daisies and long purples:
> That liberal shepherds give a grosser name;
> But our cold maids do dead men's fingers call them

The name 'orchid' comes from the round tubers that are supposed to resemble testicles, hence the shepherds' 'grosser name'. There are crowflowers (crowfoots), nettles and daisies in Millais' painting too, as well as lots of other flowers, all painted in beautiful botanical detail; in fact it's practically a virtual botany lesson.

Gardening hitchhikers

A while ago I very much enjoyed an article by Helen Dillon in which she mused on the challenges and opportunities presented by downsizing from her much-admired Dublin garden, and home of 44 years, to a smaller property. Much of the article was concerned with the plants she intends to take with her and, even more interestingly, those she plans to leave behind. Among the plants she's had enough of is the purple-leaved lesser celandine, *Ficaria verna* 'Brazen Hussy', although she admits that it will probably hitch a lift on some plant or other and turn up in the new garden, whether she likes it or not.

I sympathise; during my recent move from one end of the country to the other, I brought a few plants with me. Not very many, mainly because I knew that in the short term there was nowhere to put them, but even so I was impressed by how many unintended hitchhikers I had also brought with me. These include foxgloves, forget-me-nots, opium and Welsh poppies, dog violets and assorted aquilegias. These can be fairly described as the usual suspects: plants that produce abundant seeds, and often form a substantial part of the garden soil seed bank – at least, that part of it that doesn't consist of weeds. It's hard to say whether my plants travelled as seeds and germinated on arrival, or as young seedlings; probably a bit of both.

Another of my hitchhikers deserves a special mention, but first a small digression is required. Long ago, Steve Furness and I shared a lab while doing our PhDs at Sheffield University. Steve now runs a rather splendid alpine garden and nursery in the village of Calver, a few miles from Sheffield. If you ever visit the Peak District (as you certainly should), I strongly recommend you pay a visit.

While returning from a walk in the national park, I would occasionally drop in at Steve's nursery to say hello. On one of these occasions, Steve scraped some green stuff off a lump of tufa and said 'Here, have some of this'. 'This' turned out to be *Mentha requienii*, by far the smallest and also most charming of the mints; a native of Italy, Sardinia and Corsica, it's usually known as Corsican mint. Barely 1cm tall, it bears a superficial resemblance to mind-your-own-business (*Soleirolia soleirolii*), but is a superior plant in every way, with tiny mauve flowers and a pungent mint smell.

I forget where I put this gift when I got home, but it hardly matters; Corsican mint is one of the great colonists, both by fragments of plant and numerous tiny seeds. It soon colonised my entire garden, popping up in gravel, paving and even the veg plot. It's also moved on to my son's garden, and we can both guess where he got it from. So no real surprise that it's accompanied me to my new home in Devon, where I'm sure it will be even happier (if that's possible) than it was in Sheffield.

The final thing to say about all these plants is that they are very welcome. They're old friends, and like all old friends, I'm glad they decided to come along.

Popular flowers

A year or two ago, DIY chain Homebase carried out a survey of the garden flowers that are most attractive to house-hunters, and which therefore might help to sell your house. I've no idea exactly how the list was arrived at, but the top ten – in order – were roses, lavender, fuchsia, tulips, sweet peas, lilies, jasmine, geraniums (maybe they mean pelargoniums), hydrangea and sunflowers.

The list prompts two questions. The first is how closely this corresponds to what we actually grow in our gardens. To answer that, we can look at a recent survey of a representative sample of gardens in five UK cities (Belfast, Cardiff, Edinburgh, Leicester and Oxford). Because the survey recorded everything, I'm obviously going to ignore weeds (dandelions are very popular), and plants that aren't exactly weeds, but might as well be (for example, ivy).

Of the plants in the Homebase list, only roses, fuchsia, lavender, hydrangea and lilies are in the top 38 plants we actually grow (the rest of the top 50 are weeds). At the very top, the two lists agree: roses are found in more gardens than any other plant. But after that, it's all downhill. The next most frequently grown garden plants are montbretia, aquilegia, foxglove, fuchsia, honeysuckle, cotoneaster, mint, leylandii, clematis, apple, *Euonymus fortunei* and hebe. Only one of those (fuchsia) is in the Homebase top ten, but I think the two most surprising omissions from the latter are honeysuckle and clematis. Both are actually widely grown and surely have great home-enhancing potential; their absence suggests (despite the presence of jasmine) a widespread distrust of perennial climbers among home-buyers.

The second question is whether the list suggests that Britain's home-sellers know what they are doing. I'm not sure it does. As any estate agent will tell you, spring is far and away the best time to sell your house. People have recovered from Christmas, days are lengthening, the weather is warming up, and – crucially – buyers are about. It's also a good time in the garden: there's lots in flower, and even if your garden has a tendency to look a bit overgrown later in the year (like mine), it will still look tidy.

And yet, the Homebase list is conspicuously short of spring flowers – really only tulips. In truth, for the astute vendor, tulips are the ultimate secret weapon. However dull your garden normally is, in fact even if you don't like gardening, start your spring campaign by buying a sack of tulips the previous autumn and planting them all, anywhere you can find a bit of spare ground. Bung some in pots too, especially in the front garden. The following spring, potential buyers will be impressed by the show, and won't care at all that it consists entirely of tulips – the first impression is all that matters.

The rest of the Homebase list has a summer feel to it, and some (sunflower and hydrangea, for example) are positively autumnal. Not that that's necessarily a bad thing. Summer itself (mid-July to early September) is a bad time to sell, but autumn is second only to spring. For an autumn campaign, I don't think there's anything with quite the instant appeal of tulips in spring, but you could try dahlias. If the campaign succeeds, you won't even need to lift and store them – let the new owners worry about that.

With a longer-term eye on a spring sale, I suggest a few things that aren't in the Homebase top ten: magnolia, rhododendron, lilac, forsythia, fruit trees (apple or pear), cherry, flowering dogwood, amelanchier, flowering currant, peonies and iris. Squeeze all those in, and don't forget the tulips, and your house will sell itself.

Why weather forecasts are mostly wrong

We're all obsessed by the weather, and gardeners more than most. Half the time we are hoping it will rain so we don't have to water the veg plot, the other half we are hoping the rain will stop so we can get out and mow the lawn. So how useful are weather forecasts in helping us decide what to expect – specifically, whether it's going to rain or not?

Helpfully, the Met Office has a web page that asks 'How accurate are our public forecasts?'. Less helpfully, it reports their rain-forecasting accuracy as follows: '0.589 Equitable Threat Score (ETS) of three hourly weather is correctly forecast as "rain" on the current day.'

Pardon? Equitable what? Don't worry, they really are trying to be helpful, they just aren't trying very hard. The problem is that just reporting how often it rains when the weather man says it will isn't very useful, because that ignores the underlying probability of rain. To take an extreme example, in an equatorial rain forest I can say with complete confidence that it will rain tomorrow. But that tells you precisely nothing about my rain-forecasting skills, because it rains every day.

A legendary example of the opposite extreme is forecasting of tornadoes in the American Midwest in the late 19th century by one Sergeant John Finley. Finley claimed his twice-daily tornado forecasts were 96.6% correct. Which sounds terrific, until you consider that tornadoes are actually rare. Essentially Finley arrived at such a high success rate by being very good at forecasting the non-appearance of a non-tornado. In fact, as critics pointed out, tornadoes are so rare that Finley could have increased his forecasting accuracy to 98.2% by simply forecasting no tornado every time.

What we want is a forecasting measure that takes account of the underlying probability of whatever is being forecast. The Equitable Threat Score is one such measure. I'll spare you (and me) the maths, but the ETS is 'equitable' because it adjusts for the 'cheating' that occurs if we just forecast more of whatever happens most often. It's answering the question 'how often did it rain when the Met Office said it would, after allowing for forecasts that would have been right by chance?'.

So is an ETS of 0.589 any good? Actually it's not bad at all, and the Met Office is one of the world's best weather forecasters. But there's no getting around the problem that although rain is a lot more likely than a tornado, it still doesn't rain all that often, even in Britain. Obviously there's a lot of regional variation, but the average for the whole country, on an hourly timescale, is that the probability of rain is about 8%. In other words, if you choose 1,000 hours of weather at random, about 80 of them will be wet.

Let's assume, for the sake of argument, that the Met Office forecasts rain with about 90% accuracy, which sounds pretty good to me. That means that 90% of those 80 wet hours (72 hours) would be forecast correctly. Similarly, the forecast for 90% of the remaining 920 dry hours would also be right; these 828 hours would be correctly forecast to be dry. So far so good, but that leaves 92 hours (920-828) of dry weather that would be forecast to be wet. Which means that rain would be forecast for 164 hours (92+72) in every thousand, but rain would actually fall in only 72 of those hours. In other words, forecasts of rain are right less than half the time, even if rain really is forecast with 90% accuracy.

What does all this mean for gardeners? Looking on the bright side, it's forecasts of rain that are most likely to be wrong, so such a forecast should not deter you from getting out either the watering can or the lawnmower.

The weeds we deserve

I wrote recently that if you move from Sheffield to Devon, as I have, everything changes. But one change could easily be just as large if you moved only a few doors down the same street: your garden's history, and what that means for its plants and (especially) its weeds.

In a book on weeds nearly ten years ago, I wrote:

I read somewhere that by the time we're 40, we all have the face we deserve. That is, if you smile a lot, your face will naturally relax into cheerful creases, but if you're always miserable, you'll look miserable whether you are

255

or not. Much the same applies to weeds. The fussy, tidy gardener, forever hoeing, mowing and pruning, will be troubled only by the nimble, small-seeded, annual weeds that need the bare earth created by all that activity.

The laissez-faire gardener, in contrast, will be a prey to all the big, rhizomatous perennial weeds that thrive on neglect. Therefore he or she will have the worse weeds, but will worry about them less.

In other words, ye shall know them by their weeds, and I'm still sure that's true, but I never expected to own such a spectacular example of the phenomenon. I confess to being naturally towards the weed-phobic end of the spectrum, so my Sheffield garden was troubled mainly by the small, fast-growing weeds that are forever emerging from the seed bank (hairy bittercress, annual meadow grass) or falling out of the sky (willowherbs, dandelions). I inherited a few perennial weeds, but they were largely exterminated long ago.

My new garden couldn't be more different. It's not that its previous owners were bad gardeners, more that the possibility of gardening of any kind, apart from a handful of half-hearted roses, clearly never crossed their minds. The result is what you get when your worst weed nightmares are allowed to slug it out, in an uninterrupted bid for supremacy, for the best part of a decade. The basic fabric is thus a carpet of ground elder, mixed here and there with a sprinkling of Spanish bluebells and wood avens. As the season progresses, bindweed emerges through this blanket, some sprawling over the ground elder, some twining up the occasional moribund dwarf conifer. There's enchanter's nightshade too, which can be a serious thug in its own right, given the chance, but here it seems to struggle to cope with the competition from the ground elder and bindweed.

Looking on the bright side, I could have had couch grass and horsetail as well, while the classic weeds of disturbed ground are almost absent. In fact, if it weren't for a large patch of trampled earth around and under the former site of a children's trampoline, bittercress might not be present at all. For those who are kept awake at night by bittercress, the lesson is obvious: maintain a complete perennial cover and the problem is solved – although ground elder wouldn't be my first choice for bittercress control.

But my most surprising weed, and the most eloquent testament to the previously complete absence of any form of gardening, is not one but two thriving populations of bracken. In the countryside bracken can undoubtedly be a real menace, but in the confines of a modest suburban garden, it doesn't have what it takes to be a serious problem. In early summer it produces essentially a single cohort of fronds, so if you ruthlessly pull those up for a year or two, it quickly takes the hint. So hopeless is bracken as a garden weed that in D.G. Hessayon's *Pest and Weed Expert*, which contains a fairly comprehensive rogues' gallery, it fails to appear at all.

So there you have it: what could fairly be described as a challenge (and I haven't even mentioned the two rows of out-of-control leylandii, clearly with ambitions to become big trees). Wish me luck; the bracken will be easy, the ground elder may take a little longer.

What is a plant?

Last year, in an episode of the Radio 4 science/comedy chat show *The Infinite Monkey Cage*, Brian Cox asked plant biologist Professor Jane Langdale 'What is a plant?' As gardeners, we probably think we know a plant when we see one, so it was interesting to hear her reply: 'A multicellular organism that is in the lineage most closely related to green algae', which is perhaps not the answer most of us were expecting. Neither was stand-up comedian and failed horticulture student Ed Byrne, who suggested: 'Something that's alive that's not an animal.' Langdale might have been better to counter with a question of her own: 'What do you mean by a "plant"?' – if only because although her reply got a laugh, I think that would have got a bigger one.

If you mean plants as understood by gardeners, Byrne's definition isn't far out; almost all the living organisms we see every day are either plants or animals, although some are neither (e.g. fungi), as are plenty we *don't* see (bacteria, for example). But Langdale was giving a proper scientific definition of 'the green plants', which are green because they all share the same kinds of chlorophyll, plus the same storage compounds, internal cellular structures and lots of other things. They share those things because they're closely related – they're all on the same branch of the tree of life. And, with all due respect to Langdale's definition, they don't need to be multicellular. Unicellular green algae are in every important respect green plants; multicellularity is an unimportant detail.

So is that it? For gardeners, yes. Gardening is about growing multicellular green plants, because they are the only large photosynthetic organisms that have overcome all the problems of living on land. But the living world is far, far more complicated than that, and there are other organisms out there that you might well think should qualify as 'plants', in the sense of photosynthetic organisms big enough to notice without a microscope.

Animals and plants are eukaryotes (organisms whose cells contain nuclei, unlike bacteria, which don't). Eukaryotes themselves never evolved the ability to photosynthesise – they simply 'borrowed' the ability by engulfing a photosynthetic bacterium, which eventually became a chloroplast. This crucial event happened only once in the entire history of life, somewhere around a billion years ago. The direct line of descent from this event branched a very long time ago. One branch became the green plants, while the other became the red seaweeds, so there's a very good argument for calling red seaweeds plants; not only are they large and photosynthetic, they're even related (distantly) to green plants. I don't know why green plants conquered the land and red ones didn't, but if things had turned out differently, we might all be growing a version of H.G. Wells' red weed from *The War of the Worlds*.

But in another part of the evolutionary forest altogether, unrelated to green plants, animals and fungi, in fact unrelated to anything you've ever heard of, another group of organisms acquired chloroplasts 'second hand' by kidnapping a red alga, and then used them to build a big photosynthetic organism. These are the brown seaweeds.

In the sea, where green plants are only ever bit players, red and brown seaweeds are the dominant large photosynthetic organisms. They're important too; some red seaweeds have a calcareous skeleton and are important reef builders, the polysaccharide carrageenan, extracted from red seaweeds, is a billion-dollar industry, and is found in everything from ice cream to shampoo, while laver or *nori* is consumed in large amounts in sushi.

Brown seaweeds are vital parts of coastal ecosystems worldwide; they're certainly the most conspicuous life on the average British rocky shore. In some parts of the world, giant kelp forms huge underwater forests. But are they plants? Good question, but I think this is where we came in: depends what you mean by 'plant'.

What is a weed?

Have a look on the internet for definitions of a 'weed' and you will quickly discover numerous variations on 'a plant in the wrong place'. In fact ask any gardener the same question and it's odds on you'll get the same reply. But does that help you to understand weeds? Does it even make sense? Let's find out by looking at a couple of examples.

A while ago I wrote about the surprising appearance in my old garden of a twayblade, one of our commoner but less conspicuous native orchids. To my surprise, twayblade is listed in the *European Garden Flora*, but surely only for the sake of completeness. The RHS Plant Finder even lists one place you can actually buy it, but only from a specialist wildflower supplier, along with other plants that no one in their right mind would grow in a garden, such as dog's mercury and enchanter's nightshade (nice name, horrible plant).

In fact, if you were to set out to grow British native plants in your garden, ranked in order of some measure of garden-worthiness, you would be a long way down the list before you came to twayblade. Nor have I ever seen twayblade in cultivation, so I'm going to stick my neck out and say it's definitely not a plant you would expect to find in a garden. Which made it, in my garden, a plant in the wrong place. But was it a weed? I don't think so. It lacks the rapid growth, the territorial ambitions, the annoying air of entitlement, the determined persistence in the face of persecution – in short, any of the things I normally associate with a weed.

My second example is *Papaver rhoeas*, the common red cornfield poppy. A plant that is, without a shadow of a doubt, a weed, in fact almost the textbook example of a weed. The common poppy is one of a group of obligate arable weeds, plants that are so well adapted to cereal fields that they appear not to have a 'natural' habitat at all. Because such plants are confined to arable fields in northern Europe, botanists usually assume their original, 'wild' habitat must lie in the eastern Mediterranean area or south-west Asia, which is undoubtedly where they came from. But even there, many are not found outside arable fields; they may simply have been adapting to farmed habitats for so long that they can no longer live anywhere else.

It therefore follows that as far as the common poppy is concerned, if cereal fields are 'the wrong place', we have a plant that grows *only* in the wrong place, because it doesn't grow anywhere else. Far better, I think, to go along with reality and accept that for the common poppy, arable fields are where it belongs.

So there you have it. On the one hand, a plant that has turned up in the wrong place, but can't possibly be described as a weed. And on the other hand, a plant that couldn't be weedier if it tried, yet is so perfectly adapted to its one and only, weedy, cereal-field habitat that that must logically be the right place. Which all tends to suggest that 'a plant in the wrong place' is as vacuous and content-free as I always suspected. The truth is that weeds are too numerous, too diverse and simply too interesting for anything useful about them to be conveyed by a six-word soundbite.

There's a lesson for us all there, and it's one that goes well beyond gardening. Whenever you find your views on any topic seem to be perfectly captured by some glib phrase, it's always worth checking that the phrase really means what you think it does, or even if it means anything at all.

Plants are a breath of fresh air for asthma sufferers

Fresh air is good for you. Exercise is good for you. Being around plants is good for you. So, not surprisingly, gardening is good for you too. But we keep discovering more about exactly *why* and *how* plants are good for you. Exposure to the natural environment is linked to reduced risk of cardiovascular disease, better mental health, and simply living longer.

One health problem that has attracted a lot of attention is asthma, a chronic and increasingly common condition that affects over 300 million people worldwide. There is no cure and, although some risk factors are well known, reducing them isn't easy, so anything that might help would be welcome. Does exposure to the natural world protect against asthma? The evidence is mixed, and most studies suffer from one flaw or another, so a very large new study from New Zealand is welcome.

A unique database allowed the researchers to follow the health of *all* children (around 50,000) born in New Zealand in 1998 until age eighteen; the results are published in the journal *Nature Plants*. They looked for a relationship between asthma and average 'greenness' (from satellite imagery) around where the children lived, as well as how many different kinds of vegetation (e.g. parks, crops, deciduous or evergreen woodland, orchards, vineyards) there were in the neighbourhood. They also included the usual social and environmental factors that are known to influence asthma.

The results were clear: increased greenness and higher vegetation diversity were both linked to a small but significant reduction in prevalence of asthma. Of course, what these results don't tell you is *why*. The researchers' hunch, based on other research, is that both protective factors are linked to exposure to more (and more diverse) microbes. Essentially, they go for the 'hygiene hypothesis', which says that reduced early-childhood exposure to microbes mucks up children's immune responses, leading to greater susceptibility to allergic diseases like asthma. Consistent with the hygiene hypothesis, the results also showed that having more siblings, which is known to increase exposure to a greater variety of microbes, reduced the incidence of asthma.

It's possible that living somewhere greener simply reduces your exposure to air pollution, but the data show this is unlikely, since direct measures of air pollution, such as road density and nitrogen dioxide levels, were unrelated to asthma. Are all plants linked to lower asthma? Nearly, but not quite. Living near pine plantations actually made asthma slightly worse, probably because pine pollen can be an important respiratory allergen in sensitive individuals.

A final point to bear in mind is that the protective power of plants against asthma may be greater than revealed by this study. The data were collected, and therefore inevitably analysed, at the scale of about a city block, which conceals a lot of important detail. Maybe making your own *personal* space greener and more diverse is even better for you; in short, if you want to live a healthier and longer (and dare I say happier) life, you know what to do: get gardening.

Do healthy brains need trees?

How your brain develops is linked to the environment you experience. Studies show clearly that rats' brains fail to develop normally if they are kept in cages with the essentials for life – food, water and bedding – but nothing else. For proper brain development, rats need an 'enriched environment', which means larger cages with toys, running wheels, and ideally some company.

So far, so reasonable. But what, if any, are the lessons for human brain development? What kind of 'enriched environment' do *we* need for healthy brains? On the one hand, the classic hamster wheel seems like quite a good metaphor for modern city life, so maybe cities provide an enriched environment? On the other hand, maybe not; plenty of studies show that rural life is generally linked to better mental health.

To try to get to the bottom of all this, German researchers looked at the brains of 341 older (mostly retired) residents of Berlin. Their results were published in the journal *Scientific Reports*. Using MRI scanning, they looked at three regions of the brain, including the amygdala, which regulates the response to fear, anxiety and stress. They then looked for any connection between indicators of 'structural integrity' (a measure of normal, healthy development) of the amygdala and features of the environment near where the study subjects lived. Specifically, how much woodland, water (lakes, rivers, canals), wasteland and urban green space there was within a 1km radius of home. Green space may include trees, but was mainly parks, gardens and fields, while woodland was anywhere with tree canopy greater than 30% and tree height greater than five metres.

The results were very clear, and also a bit surprising. A healthy amygdala was linked to more nearby woodland, but not to any other land use types. In case living near woodland was related to being better off, they included the subjects' income in the analysis and found it made no difference to their results.

The reason these results are slightly surprising is that plenty of other studies have shown that improved well-being is linked to experience of green space; but here measurable effects on brain structure were linked specifically to woodland, so why should that be? It's possible that something else linked to woodland is what actually makes you feel better, such as less noise or lower air pollution. On the other hand, there is evidence that woodland itself has direct beneficial and calming effects on the brain. Japanese research has shown that *Shinrin-yoku* ('forest bathing' or 'taking in the atmosphere of the forest': basically walking in or just contemplating woodland) leads to lower salivary cortisol (reduced stress) and reduced activity in the prefrontal cortex (greater relaxation).

Like much interesting research, all this raises at least as many questions as it answers. For example, if green space with a few trees doesn't work as well as woodland, how many trees *do* you need? And how does woodland compare with other kinds of 'wild' landscape that are harder to come by in cities, such as mountains or seaside?

But from a gardening perspective, if just *looking* at some trees is good for your brain, think how much better actually *planting* one or two might be.

ANSWERS TO QUESTIONS
ON PP. 230–233

1. False
2. a
3. b
4. d
5. a
6. False
7. b
8. c
9. d
10. a
11. a

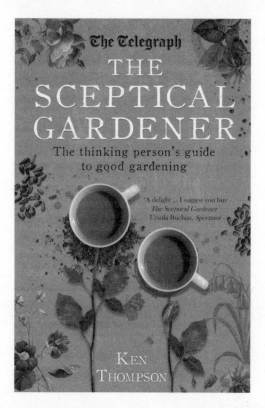